EDUCATION AND OPPORTUNITY

INQUIRY INTO CRUCIAL AMERICAN PROBLEMS
Series Editor JACK R. FRAENKEL

EDUCATION AND OPPORTUNITY:

For What and For Whom?

Second Edition

Gordon M. Seely

Professor of Education and History
San Francisco State College
San Francisco, California

PRENTICE-HALL, INC., ENGLEWOOD CLIFFS, N.J.

Photo Credits

Bruce Roberts from Rapho/Photo Researchers, Inc.: viii,46,94,104; Culver Pictures, Inc.:7; Lynn McClaren from Rapho/Photo Researchers, Inc.:20; Inger McCabe from Rapho/Photo Researchers, Inc.:26; Chester Higgins, Jr. from Rapho/Photo Researchers, Inc.:34; Paulo Koch from Rapho/Photo Researchers, Inc.:53,74; Hella Hammid from Rapho/Photo Researchers, Inc.:109.

Cover designed by Diane Kachalsky.

Library of Congress Cataloging in Publication Data
SEELY, GORDON M   1930–
    Education and opportunity.
    (Inquiry into crucial American problems)
    Bibliography: p. 000
    SUMMARY: A textbook including a short history of education in the United States and articles discussing the purpose and quality of schools, who should run them, civil liberties and the schools, and how education might be improved.
    1. Education—United States—History. 2. Segregation in education—United States—History. [1. Education—History. 2. Schools] I. Title.
LA212.S43   1976   370'.973   75-25605
ISBN 0-13-236307-0
ISBN 0-13-236299-6 pbk.

Prentice-Hall International, Inc.,
London
Prentice-Hall of Australia, Pty. Ltd.,
Sydney
Prentice-Hall of Canada, Ltd.,
Toronto
Prentice-Hall of India Private Ltd.,
New Delhi
Prentice-Hall of Japan, Inc.,
Tokyo

PREFACE

The series INQUIRY INTO CRUCIAL AMERICAN PROBLEMS focuses upon a number of important contemporary social and political issues. Each book presents an in-depth study of a particular problem, selected because of its pressing intrusion into the minds and consciences of most Americans today.

A number of divergent viewpoints, from a wide variety of different *kinds* of sources, encourage discussion and reflection, and help students to realize that the same problem may be viewed from a number of different vantage points. Of major concern throughout is a desire to help students realize that honest individuals may differ in their views.

After a short introductory chapter, Chapter Two presents a brief historical and contemporary background on the central issue. The chapters that follow explore the issue in detail. A conscientious effort has been made to avoid endorsing any one viewpoint as the "right" viewpoint, or to judge the arguments of particular individuals or organizations. Conclusions are not drawn for students. Instead, a variety of positions are presented, along with open-ended questions and involving activities, so that students can arrive at and evaluate their own conclusions.

Great care has been taken to make these books substantive, highly interesting to students, and readable. Whenever possible, dialogues involving or descriptions showing actual people responding and reacting to problematic situations are presented. Briefly, each book

- presents divergent, conflicting views on the issue under consideration;

- gives as many perspectives and dimensions on the issue as space permits;

- presents articles on a variety of reading levels;

- deals with real people involved in situations of concern to them;

- includes questions which encourage thought about and discussion of the various viewpoints expressed;

- includes activities that involve students and lead to further consideration of the problems presented;

- provides cartoons, photographs, and other illustrations to help students arrive at a more complete understanding of the issue under study.

JACK R. FRAENKEL
Series Editor

CONTENTS

1
INTRODUCTION

Schools and education are making front-page headlines these days as never before. Consider the following reports from around the United States:
From Boston, Massachusetts:

6 BOSTON SCHOOLS CLOSED AFTER ANTI-BUSING PARADE

Fearing for the safety of black students and teachers, officials yesterday emptied six South Boston schools after 8,000 whites staged a boisterous anti-busing parade down the main street of the racially troubled neighborhood.

As thousands of white students heeded a call for a one-day school boycott, officials reported the first stabbing incident since a court-ordered busing plan to integrate the city's schools was implemented. . . .

(United Press, October 5, 1974)

From Newark, New Jersey:

SEX DISCRIMINATION SUIT

The attorney for a girl who won't be allowed to graduate from high school because she failed a written test in badminton said he would file sex discrimination charges.

Attorney Joseph Buckley of the Rutgers Legal Aid Clinic said Sharon Pinkham of Spotswood, N. J., was told Friday by South River High School officials she could not get her diploma because she failed the written exam in badminton and failed to take a written test in tennis, tests not given to boys.

From Pipestone, Minnesota:

STUDENT SUES OVER SUSPENSION

Dennis Aanenson, an 18-year-old Pipestone High School student, is suing the school for suspending him from extracurricular activities because he was seen drinking—legally—in a local tavern.

The suit questions whether schools can regulate the after-school conduct of 18-year-olds, who were given adult status last year.

1

A teacher reported Aanenson after he saw him drinking beer last November in a local bar.

(Associated Press, January 28, 1974)

From New York, New York:

COLLEGE GRADUATES GETTING EDUCATION

Too late, the majority of college graduates are discovering that it no longer pays for them to go to college. Most of them "aren't likely to get into graduate schools or find jobs," says investigative reporter Roger Rapoport, who reports that 24 percent of all American freshmen want to be doctors, lawyers, or teachers because, "against all evidence," they believe these professions are "secure."

The cold facts of life after college are frightening. According to the *Esquire* study, 41,000 applicants are competing for 14,400 medical openings; 86,000 applicants are competing for 38,500 law-school openings (one top-rated law school had 3,800 applications for 290 places), [and there are] "equivalent proportions of applicants to many other graduate program places." . . .

(Wire Service Report, San Mateo *Times,* August 19, 1974)

From Sacramento, California:

GOVERNOR REAGAN SCUTTLES CAMPUS SMOKING BILL WITH VETO

A controversial bill that would have allowed high schools to set aside special areas for student smoking . . . was vetoed yesterday by Governor Ronald Reagan.

The bill had barely passed both Senate and Assembly . . . .

Reagan, a non-smoker, said he had to "wrestle with my conscience" before vetoing the bill.

"The bill was intended to correct the present situation in which students smoke in school restrooms, creating a problem for non-smoking students wishing to make use of those facilities," Reagan said in his veto message. "With only an occasional exception, high school students as an age group are prohibited by law from purchasing tobacco. It therefore seems that a far more sensible answer to solving the problem would be for school administrators to enforce a 'no-smoking' rule on school property—period," said Reagan, who used to smoke but quit years ago. . . .

(Redwood City *Tribune,* July 13, 1974)

From Detroit, Michigan:

STRIKES HIT U.S. SCHOOLS

More than 5,300 teachers went on strike in Michigan Tuesday and scattered strikes hit other school systems from New England to Washington State.

Nearly 74,000 students were idled by strikes in Detroit's suburban Wayne County, and 19,335 students had no teachers in Ann Arbor, Mich., either. In Detroit's suburban Macomb County, about 21,300 students were affected by a strike. Other, smaller strikes were reported across the state.

(The San Mateo *Times,* Sept. 4, 1974)

From Charleston, West Virginia:

THREE ARRESTED IN TEXTBOOK PROTEST

Three men, including a minister, were arrested yesterday for trying to block school buses in connection with a week-long protest over the use of textbooks that demonstrators claim are anti-Christian and immoral. Boycotts by parents who kept their children out of class and demonstrations by pickets have cut attendance in the 44,800-pupil Kanawha School District by an average of 20 percent during the week.

(Associated Press, September 7, 1974)

America's schools are the center of interest, argument, and disagreement. Parents often battle hotly to improve their children's educational opportunities. Teachers, sensitive to their professional rights and responsibilities, demand a greater voice in the control of the conditions necessary for teaching and learning. Young people, also concerned, rebel in many places against established educational practices and procedures. Educational psychologists challenge teaching methods and procedures. School administrators, bewildered by these many pressures, seek guidelines for action. And a multitude of vested interest groups, each pursuing its own desires, seek to provide such guidelines.

Critics of the schools touch on every aspect of education. Some argue, as in the cartoon below, that the entire educational system is at fault.

Others state that the schools cost too much, some that the schools are subverting American youth. The National Council for American Education,

"It's not me, Dad. It's the system that failed."

© Dow Jones, permission
The Wall Street Journal.

for example, published during the 1950s a pamphlet entitled, "They Want Your Child." It stated that the schools "were founded to preserve the American form of government and the American institutions of freedom and individual liberty. It can safely be asserted that ninety per cent of the texts and teachers in our schools today are in considerable measure subversive of these basic American principles." Several syndicated columnists lent support to this fear of subversion. How do you suppose that parents today would respond to the following remarks which appeared in newspapers from coast to coast in 1951:

> You need to know what a teacher believes. The teacher says that it is none of your business. The teacher says that the Constitution, under the Fifth Amendment, protects a citizen in his beliefs. That is absolutely true. A citizen can believe anything he likes: That the moon is made of green cheese, that Karl Marx is as great an historic figure as Moses, Jesus, Aristotle, and Plato; that John Dewey was the greatest philosopher of all time. That is a teacher's private business . . . No child need be sent to a school whose teachers offend a parent's beliefs. The child must have a certain amount of "education," according to the law. That may require the parents to pay for the upkeep of two schools. Many do.[1]

The fear that the public schools are leading us down the road to socialism and godlessness has led some critics to argue that the public schools should be abolished. Many of these people viewed with alarm the decision of the United States Supreme Court in *Abington School District v. Schempp* (1963), in which the Court banned Bible reading and the use of the Lord's Prayer in the public schools as contrary to the First Amendment. One Congressman at that time reputedly stated that the Court, in so acting, had aided "cynics, atheists, and unbelievers," to "outlaw God, step on God, ridicule God, and deny God in our public institutions."[2]

However, an attempt to bring about a reversal of the Court's decision through a Constitutional amendment met with considerable opposition, particularly from the legal profession. The Dean of the Law School of Harvard University, for example, expressed the following sentiments about tinkering with the Bill of Rights:

> To amend them here, and to amend them there, we will soon find good reasons for restricting this liberty or narrowing that safeguard, and will eventually wake up to find that we have lost essential safeguards which these Amendments can protect.[3]

[1]George Sokolsky, "Do You Know the Teachers? What Do Teachers Know?" *Rochester Times-Union,* December 28, 1951. Quoted in V. T. Thayer and Martin Levit, *The Role of the School in American Society* (New York: Dodd, Mead, and Co., 1966).
[2]*The Catholic Chronicle,* Toledo, Ohio, May 1, 1964. Cited in Thayer and Levit.
[3]Erwin N. Griswold, Dean of the Law School, Harvard University, in a letter addressed to Congressman Emanuel Celler, Chairman of the House Committee on the Judiciary, April 15, 1964.

This conflict of philosophies is only one of many raging in the field of education today.

A few critics have argued that today's schools are inferior to those of yesteryear, and that what is needed is a return to the methods, materials, and content used in the past. Many others, in perhaps the most devastating charge of all, have stated that today's schools are simply irrelevant to the needs and interests of today's young people. Black parents and reformers accuse the schools of perpetuating racial injustices and the status quo.

Many questions persist. What *should* be the purpose of the schools today? How about twenty years from today? *Are* the schools relevant?

The formal institutions of society help to perpetuate its culture and impress on the young the established values and ways of doing things. When a society is undergoing social change, as ours is today, formal institutions may lag behind. Thus, curriculum, teaching methods, the kind of teachers wanted and needed, and the control of education both within schools and within communities evoke discussion and even violence.

Although much education is obtained in informal settings and situations —at play, on the job, during casual conversations—it is the formal institutions of learning that concern us here.

In particular, we will consider in some detail the following questions:

1. What is the purpose of education?
2. Are conflicts over educational policy new?
3. How well do today's schools educate?
4. Who should run the schools?
5. How much control should the school exercise over individual self-expression (such as dress and behavior)?
6. In what ways might the schools be changed?
7. How might education be improved?

© 1961 United Feature Syndicate, Inc.

As you read this book, try to decide if Lucy is right.

2
SOME HISTORICAL NOTES

The intensity of conflicts about education, in the past and today, testifies to the importance that parents typically place on the way their children are prepared for adult life. It has been said that Americans view schooling as an answer to all problems and as a result expect schools to accomplish the impossible!

A history of the controversies that marked the growth of the enormous and complex school systems in America would occupy several volumes, since argument and healthy difference of opinion have characterized the story of American schooling from the earliest days. This chapter, therefore, will examine only a few issues of historical and contemporary interest, particularly those concerned with the purpose, the control, and the support of schools in American society.

The early settlers of America brought with them from Europe a number of ideas about education which they wished to transplant onto American soil. They were particularly influenced by the religious thinking of the Reformation, which required an educated clergy to spread religious standards of conduct, and a literate citizenry to receive these standards; and the humanist tradition of the Renaissance, which endorsed as an ideal an education focused on the learning of classical languages and letters.

Influenced by these ideas, the colonists, particularly the New England Puritans, sought to copy European schools as closely as possible under the frontier conditions of America. On the frontier, however, practical know-how and hard work were far more important than book learning, since chores for all existed in abundance and working hours were long.

The colonists realized that the taming of America would take considerable time and effort. A slow, leisurely development of education and educational institutions was not possible. They were especially fearful that their children, if exposed to the frontier conditions of America without education, would end up as barbarians. Education to prevent this was considered a necessity, and schools were rapidly established. As early as 1635, Boston voted to establish a school to be supported by the income received from a parcel of land set aside for that purpose.

The colonial school, however, played but a limited role in the education of most youngsters. Most children had only a casual brush with reading,　　**7** writing, and arithmetic in formal classrooms as we know them today. They received most of their education at home, at work, in church, and in the community at large. A clear difference existed between education, in general, and schooling, in particular.

The dominant motive for the establishment of schools during the colonial period was to provide for religious instruction. Elementary schools concentrated on teaching students to read the Bible; men who were intellectually inclined read the classics in order to understand the Scriptures more fully. Frontier conditions offered little time for the development of wide-ranging intellectual interests, and education was typically narrow in scope and meager in content. Bright students could master in a year all that an elementary school had to offer!

Most colonial American communities held a number of religious and other important beliefs in common. Schools tended to reflect these beliefs directly in the curriculum and in the materials which they used for instruction. In *The New England Primer,* for example, the title page was as follows: "The New England Primer, or an easy and pleasant guide to the art of reading, to which is added the Catechism." The readings in this chapter illustrate some of these early attitudes of Americans toward education.

---

1. The New England Primer*

Religious jingles were used to teach the children the alphabet as the first step in learning to read. Printers often improvised their own verses. Can you add verses for some additional letters to those below?

A In Adam's Fall
We sinned all.

H Heaven to find,
the Bible mind.

C Christ crucify'd
For sinners dy'd.

T Time cuts down all
both great and small.

W Whales in the sea
God's voice obey.

What Do You Think? _____

If a primer were written today, what themes might be used?

---

*From Clifton Johnson, *Old-Time Schools and School-Books* (New York: Dover Publications, 1963).

8

2. "What Will Be Your Condition in Hell?"*

The Evangelical Primer, *an expanded reader in the style of* The New England Primer, *won the praise of men like Noah Webster. A sample reading, with clear implications for both body and soul, follows:*

What will be your condition in hell? I shall be dreadfully tormented. . . . What company will be there? Legions of devils, and multitudes of sinners of the human race. Will company afford me any comfort in hell? It will not, but will probably increase my woes.

If you should go to hell, how long must you continue there? For ever and ever.

If you should die in your sins, and God should make you miserable, should you have any reason to complain of him? Not the least. I must be speechless.

What Do You Think? ————————————————

What does this reading tell you about what colonial schoolmen considered important?

3. The "Ould Deluder, Satan"†

As time went on, the educational significance of the colonial family declined, and schools became more important. In legislation passed in 1642 and in 1647 the General Court of Massachusetts sought to compel communities to provide for the education of youngsters neglected by parents. Here is a brief excerpt from the Massachusetts Law of 1647.

It being one chief project of that ould deluder, Satan, to keepe men from the knowledge of the Scriptures, . . .

It is therefore ordered, that every towneship in this jurisdiction, after the Lord hath increased them to the number of 50 householders, shall forthwith appoint one within their towne to teach all such children as shall resort to him to write and reade, whose wages shall be paid either by the parents or masters of such children, or by the inhabitants in generall.

*From Clifton Johnson, *Old-Time Schools and School-Books* (New York: Dover Publications, 1963).

†Excerpted from David B. Tyack, *Turning Points in American Educational History* (Waltham, Mass.: Blaisdell Publishing Company, 1967).

1. Why do you suppose the magistrates of Massachusetts Bay blamed "that ould deluder"?
2. What arguments might be us:d today to justify spending money for schools?

---

4. The Advancement of Learning

The colonists were not only concerned with the lower schools, however. Higher education in New England also received the attention and support of the community, from the earliest beginnings of the Massachusetts Bay Colony. An unusually large number of the colonists who came to Boston and the surrounding towns had degrees from Cambridge or Oxford, or had at least studied at one or the other.

Almost nothing was heard at the time about the impracticality of an English Renaissance curriculum in the American wilderness. No one urged that schooling be "relevant." The Renaissance curriculum of classical languages and mathematics was viewed for both vocational preparation and for liberal study. Only clergymen learned their "trade" in schools.

Richard Mather, in *New England's First Fruits*, in 1643 set forth the dual purpose of Harvard and of all American higher education for the next one hundred years. Would you agree with Puritan priorities?

> After God had carried us safe to New England, and we had builded our houses, provided necessaries for our livelihood, reared convenient places for God's worship, and settled the civil government, one of the next things we longed for was to advance learning and perpetuate it to posterity; dreading to leave an illiterate ministry to the churches, when our present ministers shall lie in the dust.[1]

As America developed into a larger and more complex society, colonial educational emphases on tradition and religious orthodoxy came under question. The earliest colonizers viewed life as stable and settled. Education, in their view, served to fit people into a preordained, fixed social structure. America, however, proved to be a land of experiment, of enormous opportunity, and of rapid material and social change. Schools, many argued, should look to the present and the future, not the past, for their aims and materials.

Benjamin Franklin was one who wanted change in schools. A man whose life had been characterized by enterprise and experiment, he proposed in 1749 a forward-looking secondary school, or academy, for Philadelphia. In this

[1]Excerpted from Perry Miller (ed.), *The American Puritans: Their Prose and Poetry* (Garden City, N.Y.: Doubleday & Company, Inc., 1956).

academy, educational tradition and religious orthodoxy were to be minimized. Franklin urged instruction in English and modern languages for all students and Latin only for those who would need it. His curriculum included such practical and needed skills as navigation and surveying, and sought to prepare young men for rapidly developing business careers as well as for the professions. Moral training, vital in Franklin's view, would be based on what he believed was just and satisfactory behavior, rather than on religious doctrine.

Franklin's school reform met serious opposition and, in his judgment, sabotage at the hands of the classical scholars. In 1789 he wrote a defense of his school plan of 1749 and a criticism of what the defenders of Greek and Latin had done to it. In attacking an over-emphasis on Latin and Greek, Franklin raised the question of whether the curriculum should be "relevant" to the needs of life. He asked the very hard question that Herbert Spencer posed some seventy years later in his essay, "What Knowledge Is of Most Worth?" The same question is frequently, and often warmly, debated today.

What Do You Think?

1. What does the short excerpt tell you about Puritan values?
2. Would you consider Franklin's school "relevant" to his time? Who might object to such an argument?

5. "The Time Spent . . . Might . . . Be Much Better Employ'd"

As you read the views of Franklin and Jefferson expressed below, ask yourself what subjects you would include or exclude from the curriculum. Why? What choice would Franklin make? Jefferson?

But there is in Mankind an unaccountable Prejudice in favour of ancient Customs and Habitudes, which [continues] them after the Circumstances, which formerly made them useful, cease to exist. A Multitude of Instances might be given, but it may suffice to mention one. Hats once were thought an useful Part of Dress.

At what Time Hats were first introduced we know not, but in the last Century, they were universally worn thro'out Europe. Gradually, however, as the Wearing of Wigs, and Hair nicely dress'd prevailed, the putting on of Hats was disused by genteel People, lest the curious Arrangements of the Curls and Powdering should be disordered . . . yet still our Considering the Hats as a part of Dress continues so far to prevail, that a Man of fashion is not thought dress'd without having one, or

11

something like one, about him, which he carries under his Arm ... a *Chapeau bras* [a small, three-cornered silk hat made to be carried under the arm], though the utility of such a mode of wearing it is by no means apparent, and it is attended not only with some expense, but with a degree of constant trouble.

The still prevailing custom of having schools for teaching generally our children, in these days, the Latin and Greek languages, I consider therefore, in no other light than as the *Chapeau bras* of modern Literature.

Thus the Time spent in that Study might, it seems, be much better employ'd in the Education for such a Country as ours.[1]

Among the founding fathers, Thomas Jefferson was the most interested in education. Less concerned with utility in education than Franklin, Jefferson argued that a republican government required widespread educational opportunities for the common people. While Governor of Virginia he prepared "A Bill for the More General Diffusion of Knowledge," which contained the elements of a public system of tax-supported education that would permit able youngsters to move from the lowest grade through the university at state expense. Jefferson conceived this system of schools as the means by which a "natural aristocracy" of talent would emerge to lead the nation.

In 1786 Jefferson wrote from Paris to his former teacher, George Wythe, his observations about French society and these frequently quoted words about education:

I think by far the most important bill in our whole code is that for the diffusion of knowledge among the people. No other sure foundation can be devised for the preservation of freedom, and happiness. If anybody thinks that kings, nobles, or priests are good conservators of the public happiness, send them here. It is the best school of the universe to cure them of that folly. ... Preach, my dear Sir, a crusade against ignorance; establish and improve the law for educating the common people. Let our countrymen know that the people alone can protect us against these evils, and that the tax which will be paid for this purpose is not more than the thousandth part of what will be paid to kings, priests and nobles who will rise up among us if we leave the people in ignorance.[2]

Other writers in young America outlined original plans for utilizing the schools to strengthen the new nation. Among them were Dr. Benjamin Rush of Philadelphia and E. I. Dupont de Nemours, French emigré and close friend of Jefferson. None of the plans, including Jefferson's, was ever fully implemented, however. Yet they contained several common ideas that would provide the basis for discussion and argument for the public school movement of

[1]Daniel Calhoun (ed.), quoted from Benjamin Franklin in *The Educating of Americans: A Documentary History* (Boston: Houghton Mifflin Co., 1969).

[2]Julian P. Boyd (ed.), *The Papers of Thomas Jefferson* (Princeton, N. J.: Princeton University Press, 1950 et seq.).

the 1830s and 1840s and that would ultimately become fundamental principles of American educational policy.

During the 1830s, when Andrew Jackson was in the White House, various states of the Union began to form tax-supported, public-controlled nonsectarian systems of schools. As politics and social affairs became more democratic, so did the schools. The guiding principle became the idea that all American youngsters should receive elementary education at public expense. After 1830, the states moved toward that goal slowly, imperfectly, and always in the face of strong opposition. Farmers argued that most school learning was useless if not corrupting and in addition deprived fathers of the much-needed labor of their children. (Echoes of that argument linger today among some religious sects of Pennsylvania and the Middle West.) Others argued that taxation for free schools was socialistic and deprived property owners unjustly of their savings. Still others declared that education was after all a private matter, the responsibility of parents, and no business of the state.

What Do You Think? _____

1. How do you suppose Franklin would react to Jefferson's ideas?
2. What groups might you expect to support the expansion of the public school system?

6. Thaddeus Stevens and the Pauper Law*

In the following selection, Thaddeus Stevens, mighty campaigner for public schools in Pennsylvania and later architect of congressional "Reconstruction," argues the merits of tax-supported, free public schools before the lower house of the Pennsylvania Legislature. His arguments are typical of the statements of many who sought a system of free schools.

Mr. Speaker, I will briefly give you the reasons why I shall oppose the repeal of the school law. . . .

If an elective Republic is to endure for any great length of time, every elector must have sufficient information, not only to accumulate wealth and take care of his pecuniary concerns, but to direct wisely the legislature, the ambassadors, and the Executive of the nation—for some part of all these things, some agency in approving or disapproving of them, falls to every freeman. If then, the permanency of our Government depends upon such

*Excerpted from Thaddeus Stevens, Speech to the Pennsylvania Legislature, 1835, *Report of the United States Commissioner of Education for 1898–1899*, pp. 518–521.

knowledge, it is the duty of government to see that the means of information be diffused to every citizen. This is a sufficient answer to those who deem education a private and not a public duty—who argue that they are willing to educate their own children, but not their neighbor's children. . . .

This law is often objected to, because its benefits are shared by the children of the profligate spendthrift equally with those of the most industrious and economical habits. It ought to be remembered that the benefit is bestowed, not upon the erring parents, but the innocent children. Carry out this objection and you punish children for the crimes or misfortunes of their parents. You virtually establish castes and grades founded on no merit of the particular generation, but on the demerits of their ancestors; an aristocracy of the most odious and insolvent kind—the aristocracy of wealth and pride.

It is said that its advantages will be unjustly and unequally enjoyed, because the industrious, money-making man keeps his whole family constantly employed, and has but little time for them to spend at school; while the idle man has but little employment for his family, and they will constantly attend school. I know, sir, that there are some men, whose whole souls are so completely absorbed in the accumulation of wealth, and whose avarice so increases with success, that they, as well as the ox and the ass within their gates, are valuable only in proportion to their annual earnings. And, according to the present system, the children of such men are reduced almost to an intellectual level with their co-laborers of the brute creation. This law will be of vast advantage to the offspring of such misers. If they are compelled to pay their taxes to support schools, their very meanness will induce them to send their children to them to get the worth of their money. Thus it will extract good out of the very penuriousness of the miser. Surely a system which will work such wonders, ought to be as greedily sought for, and more highly prized, than that coveted alchemy which was to produce gold and silver out of the blood and entrails of vipers, lizards, and other filthy vermin.

What Do You Think?————————————————————————

How relevant are Steven's major arguments in behalf of tax-supported schools to controversy today over the high cost of schools?

7. Opposition to Public Schools

Much determined opposition to public schools came from parents concerned with the control of such schools. Some parents feared that the exclusion of religion from public schools would result in a godless education; others feared that if religion were taught in the public schools, the effect would be harmful to minority sects in a given community. In either case, parents insisted upon the God-given right to control the religious education of their children.

No group in the 1840s felt more strongly about the importance of religious training in the education of children than did the Roman Catholics, who frequently opposed public schools as being in effect Protestant schools. In the City of New York, Bishop John J. Hughes, a vigorous and militant churchman, sought to preserve the earlier practice of legislative grants of money to private school societies, secular and religious. His arguments and those of the Methodists, whom he sought to answer, follow:

Address to the Alderman of Bishop John J. Hughes, October 29, 1840

We have been driven, by the obligation of our consciences, and at our expense which we are poorly able to bear—to provide schools; but they are not convenient, they are not well ventilated, and are not well calculated to give that development to your young citizens which they ought to have. [Bishop Hughes then traced the history of public help to private school societies, which he claimed had resulted in good education for the needy and permitted the development in youngsters of conscience solidly grounded on religious principle.] It should be taught that here [in developing conscience] neighbors have the right to differ, and whatever is the right of one must be recognized as the right of the other; and the distribution [to church schools] of this [school] fund will be better calculated to benefit the community than it can be by these public schools, where everything seems to be at par except religion, and that is below par at an immense discount.

A Committee of Methodist Pastors Protest

It must be manifest to the Common Council, that, if the Roman Catholic claims are granted [claims for state aid to Catholic schools], all the other Christian denominations will urge their claims for a similar appropriation, and that the money raised for education by a general tax will be solely applied to the purposes of proselytism, through the medium of sectarian schools. But if this were done, would it be the price of peace? or would it not throw the apple of discord into the whole Christian community? . . . Should we agree in the division of the spoils? Would each sect be satisfied with the portion allotted to it? . . . when all the Christian sects shall be satisfied with their individual share of the public fund, what is to become of those children whose parents belong to none of these sects, and who cannot conscientiously allow them to be educated in the peculiar dogmas of any one of them? . . . It must be plain to every impartial observer, that the applicants [the Catholics] are opposed to the whole system of public school instruction; and it will be found that the uncharitable exclusiveness of their creed must ever be opposed to all public instruction which is not under the direction of their own priesthood. . . . We are sorry that the reading of the Bible in the public schools, without note or commentary, is offensive to them; but we cannot allow the Holy Scriptures to be accompanied with *their* notes and commentaries.[1]

[1]Above excerpts from William Oland Bourne, *History of the Public School Society of the City of New York* (New York, 1870).

What Do You Think?

1. Do public schools discriminate against religion by excluding such study from the curriculum? Is religious neutrality in effect the same thing as "godlessness"?
2. Could Catholics in the 1840s reasonably argue that the nonsectarian public schools of New York City were indeed Protestant schools? If so, why?
3. What are the merits of state grants today to private schools? What are the problems with such proposals?

8. Free Education Is Extended

Prior to the Civil War, free elementary schools were well established in the North and West; following the struggle, Southern states moved to develop similar systems for their children.

As America rapidly industrialized, the education provided by parents and elementary schools was inadequate to the needs of ever-larger numbers of young people. Pressure for free secondary education began to mount. Arguments similar to those heard against taxation for free elementary schools were repeated. In what became known as the Kalamazoo case, the Michigan Supreme Court set a precedent by its ruling that taxes could be levied to provide free secondary-level schooling, thus extending the principle of public-supported schools. The conclusion of the Court decision follows:

> We content ourselves with the statement that neither in our state policy, in our constitution, or in our laws, do we find the primary school districts restricted in the branches of knowledge which their officers may cause to be taught, or the grade of instruction that may be given, if their voters consent in regular form to bear the expense and raise the taxes for the purpose.[1]

After this decision, secondary school enrollments rapidly mounted, and soon another issue rose to prominence: the need for a broader curriculum that would include industrial training to prepare students for the labor market. After considerable discussion by educators, spokesmen of industry, and representatives of labor unions, Congress finally passed the Smith-Hughes Act in 1917. This act provided for federal support of vocational, agricultural, and home economics programs in high schools. Ironically, even though the curriculum was now broadened to include the majority of students, who did not go on to college, the programs rapidly became obsolete and were never considered fully satisfactory. Today, the schools have been accused of neglecting this majority for the college-bound. The following excerpt reflects this view:

[1] Excerpted from *Stuart et al v. School District No. 1 of the Village of Kalamazoo,* 30 Michigan 69 (1874).

Guidance counselors pay "little or no attention" to job-oriented high school students, a Government-sponsored survey finds. The Advisory Council on Vocational Education reports that 90 per cent of U.S. high schools have academic counseling services, but only half of them offer vocational guidance. The result: Many youngsters flounder in the job market and feed the nation's high rate of teen-age unemployment.

Vocational guidance languishes because of the country's obsession with a college degree, some Government and union officials contend. Otto Pragan, an AFL-CIO education expert, complains that many educators feel that "blue-collar jobs are somehow inferior." Labor Department-sponsored studies show that some high school guidance counselors don't have any training or experience in vocational guidance.[2]

What Do You Think?

1. To what extent does a decision such as the Michigan Supreme Court rendered in the Kalamazoo case make history? To what extent does such a decision reflect the temper of the times?

2. Could the criticism raised about counseling be broadened to include parts of the curriculum of the typical high school of today? Explain.

3. Some people have suggested that industry should develop in-plant programs to include both technical-vocational and liberal training. Is this a good idea? Why or why not?

---

9. The Oregon School Case*

Another historic court case had its origins in an act of the Oregon legislature, which asserted the states' control of education by requiring the attendance of all children under sixteen in public schools. Three years later the U.S. Supreme Court struck down the Oregon law and upheld the right of the parents to exercise a free choice of schools. Excerpts from the Court's decision follow:

The challenged Act, effective September 1, 1926, requires every parent, guardian or other person having control or charge or custody of a child between eight and sixteen years to send him "to a public school for the period of time a public school shall be held during the current year" in the district where the child resides; and failure so to do is declared a misdemeanor. The manifest purpose is to compel general attendance at public schools by normal children, between eight and sixteen.

[2]Excerpted from *The Wall Street Journal,* September 16, 1969.
*Excerpted from *Pierce v. Society of Sisters,* 268 U.S. 510 (1925).

After setting out the above facts the Society's bill [The case was brought by the Society of Sisters, a Roman Catholic teaching group] alleges that the enactment conflicts with the right of parents to choose schools where their children will receive appropriate mental and religious training, the right of the child to influence the parents' choice of a school, the right of schools and teachers therein to engage in a useful business or profession, and is accordingly repugnant to the Constitution and void. . . .

No question is raised concerning the power of the State reasonably to regulate all schools, to inspect, supervise and examine them, their teachers and pupils; to require that all children of proper age attend some school, that teachers shall be of good moral character and patriotic disposition, that certain studies plainly essential to good citizenship must be taught, and that nothing be taught which is manifestly inimical to the public welfare.

The inevitable practical result of enforcing the Act under consideration would be destruction of appellees' primary schools, and perhaps all other private primary schools for normal children within the State of Oregon.

The fundamental theory of liberty upon which all governments in this Union repose excludes any general power of the State to standardize its children by forcing them to accept instruction from public teachers only. The child is not the mere creature of the State; those who nurture him and direct his destiny have the right, coupled with the high duty, to recognize and prepare him for additional obligations.

What Do You Think?

1. What were the fundamental issues raised in the Oregon case?
2. Suppose the Supreme Court had upheld the Oregon law? What would have been the consequences for education? For American society?

---

10. Control of the Schools Today

Today the issues of control and support of schools present themselves in new ways. In an increasingly technical, organized world, is a free college education the right—not merely the privilege—of young Americans? Is such a level of education in contemporary American society perhaps simply the equivalent of the elementary schooling of the 1840s?

Also—are parents secure in their right to control the education of their children if nonpublic schools cannot exist without some form of tax support? Can a right in principle that is denied in practice have any value?

In many large American cities today parents from minority groups as well as parents representing particular neighborhoods or sections of cities argue that giant-sized urban school districts make parental control of education impossible. Elected school boards in such cities, many maintain, are totally unrepresentative of parents' opinions.

In the chapters that follow, many contemporary issues in schools are outlined and debated from varying points of view. Some, like the issues of control and support, have long histories and promise to persist far into the future. Others will have less staying power. In considering any issues, however, try to make use of the historical dimension in your analysis. The Spanish philosopher Ortega y Gasset wrote, "History is a system, the system of human experiences, linked in a single, inexorable chain. Hence nothing can be truly clear in history until everything is clear." In looking forward to the opportunities of tomorrow, there may be a tendency to forget that the story of the past is also the tale of problems met and overcome.

3
WHAT IS THE PURPOSE OF EDUCATION?

What kind of education do we want? Are education and schooling the same? What is the "point" of education? Education is concerned with the development of human beings. When we discuss the kind of education we want and need, we are in fact discussing the kind of human beings we want and need in our society.

An education that develops complete human beings with no particular reference to vocation has been urged by educational philosophers from the time of Aristotle. The terms *liberal education* and *general education* have frequently been used to designate such an educational aim.

Other individuals, however, have called for an education that will prepare youngsters to take their place immediately in the world of work. With the increasing importance of a college education today, vocational education is generally urged for only a portion of America's young people. The definition of vocational education itself is changing, however, and some people insist that such training is an important function of our schools.

As you read the articles in this chapter, ask yourself: What should be the purpose of education? Should there be one or several purposes? And who is to decide what these purposes are?

1. Is This What Schools Are For?*

In this reading some students offer some rather pointed insights about the schools. Do they sound familiar?

"We go to school because it's the law." He was sixteen, intelligent, and had hair too long and eyes too wise for the comfort of either parent or teacher. "They make you stay until you are sixteen, and by then you may as well go on since you probably only have another year or two, anyway. The point of it, I guess, is to get a diploma so you can go to college." . . .

"It's pretty stupid really," [the] student went on, "Most of what you have

*Kathryn Johnston Noyes and Gordon L. McAndrew, *Saturday Review,* December 21, 1968. Copyright © 1968 Saturday Review, Inc.

to learn isn't worth the time or trouble. It's mostly memorizing, which in this day and age is so much wasted effort. Information is available everywhere, except maybe in the jungle or someplace like that. And if you were in the jungle, you wouldn't be worried about the kind of information we have to memorize. Even my little brother knows it's stupid. The other night—and he's only ten years old—he asked my mother why he had to memorize all those dates about the Civil War when we have an encyclopedia and he could look them up in five minutes any time he needed to know. She couldn't answer him." He shrugged his shoulders and laughed. "Oh, well, I won't put you on. I could give you some pretty spooky answers to what school is for, but the fact is that aside from the college thing, I really don't know. It's a system, that's all."

The interview seemed to be ended and then, quite suddenly, he began to talk again: "It's a system, you have to understand that. I guess it's because there are so many kids and they all have to be in school so many days a year for so many hours. Or maybe it's because the people who run schools finally get to the point where they don't like kids and don't want to have too much to do with them. Anyway, it's a system. It's like a machine. One person, a person like me, say, can't beat it.

"Let me tell you about it. I'm failing math and science, see? My second-year algebra teacher told me she took the exact same course I'm failing now when she was a sophomore in college. But that was a hundred years ago, and now they won't even let you in college unless you've already had it. I'm in the eleventh grade, and if I fail these two subjects, I probably won't get into college. So I look around and I see that other kids are passing them who aren't any smarter than I am. So I figure the trouble has to be with me. So I need guidance, right? I decide I should go talk with the guidance counselor.

"But you see, that's where the system comes in. The guidance counselor has the whole eleventh grade to worry about in my school—642 students. So he keeps this sign on his door: DO NOT ENTER WITHOUT AN APPOINT-MENT. I guess he's in there talking with some kid who's in trouble or something, and doesn't want to be interrupted. I go down there before school, after school, and during my lunch break. The sign is always there.

"Finally, I go to the main office and ask how I can get an appointment with the guidance counselor. The girl behind the desk, a student, looks at me like I'm not all there and says that I have to make an appointment with him, personally. I explain that I can't get into his office to make an appointment, and she says that the sign's only up before and after school and at lunch period, and that I can get into his office during study hall, if I get a pass from the main office to leave the study hall. Are you following me?

"OK, fine. The only trouble with this is, I don't have a study hall. I'm carrying a full load and I'm in some class or other all day. Well, the girl didn't know what to do about this, so she went and asked the old lady who works in the office. The old lady comes over to me and starts in again at the beginning and tells me that appointments with the guidance counselor must be made during the student's study hall. I ask her what happens if the student doesn't have a study hall, and she says that it always works out all right because students who don't have study halls don't have them because they are carrying a full load, and the only kids who are allowed to carry a full load are the smart ones who don't need the guidance counselor anyway.

"You see what I mean? You just can't beat it. It's kind of funny when I tell it like this, like a comedy of errors or an old Laurel and Hardy comedy on TV. But it's not funny to me because it's my *life*. . . . I don't know what's going to happen to me. How can I keep my sense of humor when I'm going to get ruined by a damned *system?*"

We couldn't answer his question and didn't try. He let us off the hook by shrugging again and saying, "Oh, well. My mother finally went and talked with my teachers. They don't think I'm trying. She was all right about it—I guess she's as worried as I am. But I *am* trying and I'm still failing, and God knows where it will all end."

Two thousand miles away, another boy picked up the "system" theory. This one was slicker than the first and far slyer in terms of "getting through" (a significantly universal term, by the way). "School is like roulette or something. You can't just ask: Well, what's the point of it?" he explained. "The point of it is to do it, to get through and get into college. But you have to figure the system or you can't win, because the odds are all on the house's side. I guess it's a little like the real world in that way. The main thing is not to take it personal, to understand that it's just a system and it treats you the same way it treats everybody else, like an engine or a machine or something mechanical. Our names get fed into it—*we* get fed into it—when we're five years old, and if we catch on and watch our step, it spits us out when we're seventeen or eighteen, ready for college.

"But some kids never understand this, and they get caught, chewed up, or pushed out. I'll give you an example: The other day this other guy and I had to make up an English test we'd missed because we were absent. The English teacher said she'd give it to us at 8 o'clock in the morning before school begins. Well, I knew that if the test made me late for my homeroom period at 8:30, that teacher would send down an absent slip on me to the office. So I went to my homeroom at five of 8 and wrote a note on the blackboard to the teacher, telling her where I was and that I might be late.

"This other guy, though, he didn't know enough to do that. He hasn't studied the system. So we go and make up our test and sure enough before we are through the late bell rings for homeroom period. I can see he's nervous and he doesn't know what to do, so he tries to hurry up and finish the test so he can get to his homeroom before the absent slips get sent down. He tears through the test and probably marks half the multiple-choices wrong. Then he takes off just as the first bell for first period is ringing.

"I saw him later in the day and he was all shook up. He couldn't catch the absent slips so he had to go down to the dean of boys' office to explain that he wasn't really tardy or absent. But the dean's office had a long line, and while the guy's waiting in line, the late bell for first period rings. So now he's half-way out of his mind, you know? By the time he gets up to the dean of boys, he really *is* late for first period and another absent slip about him is already on its way down from *that* teacher. The dean of boys tells him to come in for detention after school, one hour."

Our narrator stopped and laughed uproariously and then went on. "Well, the guy gets all uptight and tries to explain why he now has two absent slips going when he wasn't even tardy. He loses his cool and says some things and the dean says some things and the next thing you know, the guy's got *two* hours detention, for being rude and smart-alecky. But wait, it gets worse. I swear he hasn't got a brain, that kid. Anyway, as it happens, the day he was absent and missed the English test, he also missed a math test. And he's scheduled to make that one up after school, when he's supposed to be in the detention hall. If he misses the math test it won't be given again, and he doesn't know if his grade can stand a zero for this marking period. But if he misses detention, he might be suspended and have three days' worth of stuff to make up when he gets back.

"I don't know what he did, finally. Probably just had a nervous break-down. It was really pathetic. But the point is that he should have foreseen all that and made arrangements for it. I'll be surprised if he makes it through school. He just doesn't understand the system."

The speaker obviously did; he had learned well. The only question is, is that what he went to school to learn?

Our last example is shorter and more succinct, but it is one we heard many times, from both boys and girls. It goes like this: School was invented to bug kids.

These were high schoolers, and their stories were depressingly the same from one coast to the other. The system syndrome turns up in junior and senior high schools of all shapes and sizes and, contrary to what might be expected, seems as prevalent in relatively small schools as it is in schools with 2,000 or more students. The same two words were spoken in all the regional accents of America: *system* and *machine.*

The elementary schools are no more human in their dealings with students. Although the self-contained classroom allows more opportunity for the teacher to know her students, this is balanced by her determination to "mold" them into what she and the school authorites think they should be. And what they should be, at the end of any given year, is ready for the next year. In the final analysis, the first-grade teacher's aim is to prepare her students for the second grade, and so forth from elementary school to junior high, from junior high to college.

Generally speaking, the typical first-grader is inclined to be outgoing, uninhibited, and candid. He arrives at the schoolhouse door eager and primed for what lies ahead. If he has the verbal tools or inclination to communicate with you at all, he is likely to tell you early in your acquaintance that he goes to school now. It's a big thing in his life and, psychologically speaking, he is probably far more interested in school at this point than he ever will be again.

What happens to him next will be a series of little things, none of them especially traumatic, but all of them together sufficient to turn his enthusiasm down, if not off. By the end of first grade the child is no longer excited and proud to be a schoolboy. By now, he probably doesn't like school half as well as he likes home or the streets, and his favorite subject is recess. And the chances are that he doesn't like school very much because, somehow, he has gotten the idea that school doesn't particularly like him. He is too often corrected and reprimanded, too infrequently challenged, and too consistently bored. The exceptions to these schools that turn off their students so effectively number in the hundreds. But the American public is supporting more than 100,000 schools.

No child can think well of himself if the individuals with whom he comes in contact do not seem to think well of him; no one who thinks of himself as fodder for a machine—or a "system"—is likely to have a comfortably good opinion of himself. Simply because nobody else seems to think he matters at all, he must spend a good deal of time and energy proclaiming that he does. If he is not able to do this, if he cannot make himself believe in his own worth, he will soon be broken.

As presently organized, the inescapable truth is that our schools seldom promote and frequently deny the objectives we, as a nation, espouse. Rather than being assisted and encouraged to develop their own individuality, our children are locked into a regimented system that attempts to stamp them all in the same mold. The student is filled with facts and figures which only accidentally and infrequently have anything whatsoever to do with the problems and conflicts of modern life or his own inner concerns. What he needs and wants are matters of no apparent interest to anyone associated with the schools.

In sum, we run our schools almost totally without reference to the needs of the children who attend them. What we teach, how we teach it, and even when and where we teach it are far too often based upon the needs and convenience of the school, upon the comfort of the administrators, and the logistics of the system. And the students are all too aware of this; in all of our dozens of conversations with students in all parts of the country, not one boy or girl ever [said] . . . "The schools are for kids."

What Do You Think? ————————————————————

1. Would you agree with the charge that school is a "system"? Why?
2. Whom *should* the schools be for? Why?

2. Should the School Stick to Basics?*

In the spirited discussion concerning education in America that followed the launching of the Russian Sputnik in 1957, one of the clearest speakers for a definition of

*Excerpted from Mortimer Smith, *A Citizen's Manual for Public Schools* (Boston: Little, Brown and Company, 1965).

education in largely intellectual terms was the Council for Basic Education. Is the definition that follows adequate to today's needs? How would you respond to this argument?

To revert to the question of what basic education in the schools means: the first necessity is to decide what the primary purpose of schools is. The school has, of course, many subsidiary purposes, but the Council for Basic Education believes that its primary purpose is fourfold: (1) to teach young people how to read and write and figure; (2) to transmit the facts about the heritage and culture of the race; (3) in the process of (1) and (2) to train the intelligence and to stimulate the pleasures of thought; and (4) to provide that atmosphere of moral affirmation without which education is merely animal training. In the words of the educator, I. L. Kandel, the school is the place for "making the child literate in the essential fields of human knowledge."

* * * * *

To sum up, this should be the *bare minimum* expected of a normal child finishing the elementary school: He should be able to read and write with some fluency, and spell, add, subtract, multiply, and divide with accuracy; he should know the basic geographical facts of his country and the world; have a knowledge of elementary science, know something of the culture and history of other people and much of his own. And above all, his schooling should have taught him the difference between aimless mental activity and orderly thought.

* * * * *

Speaking again in terms of a bare minimum, this should probably be a program not only for the above average but for the average student as well: English (literature, composition, grammar) throughout the four years (of the high school); at the very least, two years of history; a year of plane geometry and one of elementary algebra, an opportunity to select advanced math; a year of biology, and one of a physical science; some foreign languages for all, much for the college bound; music and art as electives; and physical education properly subordinated to the academic program. This, or a similar program, should be the basic curriculum in a high school—academic, business or vocational.

* * * * *

In summing up the meaning of basic education, it is well to recall two remarks of A. N. Whitehead, who said that education is a patient process of the mastery of details, and that the problem of education is to make the pupil see the wood by means of the trees. The school should be a place where the individual learns to know the trees so well he will be able in later years, in college or in the world, to see the beauty of the forest.

What Do You Think? _____

1. Do you believe the author has described an adequate program for Americans today? Why or why not? What would you add or delete?

2. If the schools did what Mr. Smith suggests, would other agencies have to be strengthened to meet current social needs? If so, which ones? Could it be that in the case of something like driver training that the Department of Motor Vehicles could do a better job of teaching than the schools? Explain your reasoning.

3. "A Liberal Education Has Nothing To Do with Immediate Productivity"*

Here is another view as to the purpose of education. What would the author of the previous reading say to this?

Unemployment used to be a scary word, but somewhere in the affluent 60s and 70s it changed its tune.

Today, while jobs go begging, a new leisure class of "significant numbers" has adopted chronic unemployment as a lifestyle, said Michael J. Welsh, public relations officer of the . . . Hawaii Employment Association.

Welsh said HEA member firms, which handle about 80 percent of private agency job placements, report more work opportunities than people seeking them.

Or if they're seeking, some are under-educated to fill the available jobs. Others are over-educated in fields which offer few jobs. Whatever the problem, Welsh said there is a great shying away from available work which job seekers consider routine or "unchallenging."

An applicant told him, "If you can find me something for about $15,000 a year, kind of challenging, about 20 to 25 [work] hours a week, let me know."

Another, an Ivy League college graduate who Welsh said could have gone into a sales job and advanced to an administrative position, was making $1,400 a month as a parking valet at a Waikiki restaurant.

"He didn't want to leave the parking job at the time," Welsh said. "I don't know where he is now. . . ."

Welsh said today's unemployment statistics, which he doesn't expect to drop below 4 or 5 percent, are partly the result of attitude and partly caused by a flaw in education.

"We're producing record numbers of people with college and graduate degrees and a lot of them are having trouble finding jobs in their fields.

"Possibly the education system is going a little overboard. They feel it's mentally challenging [to get a degree] but they don't stop to ask, 'How much demand is there for a degree holder in this profession?' But it's costing the taxpayer to get students through these programs.

"Maybe we should ask, 'What is the education system for?'

"Is it to produce someone capable of productively entering the economic scene? Or is the purpose merely to provide education for his own self-satisfaction and mental stimulation?

"If it's the former, it is of benefit to everyone. If it's the latter, why should the taxpayer bear the burden?

*Mary Cooke, "New Leisure: Unemployment as a Lifestyle," *The Honolulu Advertiser,* June 20, 1974.

"A liberal education is fine. It stimulates and it's an enjoyable way to get an education. But a liberal education has nothing to do with immediate productivity.

"There are people with high school diplomas or college degrees who have no real skill or experience. The high schools don't really point them in any direction but there are a lot of different ways to go.

"The community colleges and business colleges offer good programs and technical skills. People in accounting and bookeeping should have no trouble [finding jobs] if they take the educational part seriously. With technical education you're into immediate dollar productivity."

Welsh's message to high school and college graduates is: Find out what is available in the job market and decide on a goal. He advises beginners to "take a lesser job to develop skills and experience."

"But they say they don't want that. They want something more challenging. They're impatient. They don't want to work up through the ranks.

"One problem, somewhere in the education process they have been told that every job should be extremely meaningful and challenging. The fact is, every job has a certain amount of routine connected with it. ..."

What Do You Think?

1. Would you agree that "a liberal education has nothing to do with immediate productivity"? What does this mean?

2. Should taxpayers pay the burden of providing an education for people that is only "mentally stimulating" and not "economically productive"? Why or why not?

4. Education and Schooling Are Not the Same*

The author discriminates between education, skill training, and custodial care as purposes of the school, arguing that education (as he defines the term) should not be attempted by the the school. Note the careful distinctions he makes as you sample his argument. Do you agree with him?

The main intended function of schooling has been education, which in its largest sense is the deliberate development of the human personality, the making of citizens. Two other functions worthy of note are child care—simply providing a suitable place for children to be kept—and training in the basic

*Excerpted from Carl Bereiter, "Schools Without Education," *Harvard Educational Review*, 42, Summer 1972. Copyright © 1972 by President and Fellows of Harvard College.

29

skills of literacy and calculation. These two functions have been assimilated to the educational function to such an extent that they do not appear at all separable. Education without child care and training is indeed difficult to imagine, but the reverse is not. One can imagine child care facilities in which there was no deliberate attempt to influence human development but only an effort to provide a wholesome environment for children as they are. It is even easier to imagine training divorced from education, because plenty of it exists already outside the schools: training in swimming, sailing, playing musical instruments, driving, and most on-the-job training is carried out with a modesty of purpose that stops well short of any intent to educate the whole person.

. . . Schools should drop their educational function in order to do a better job of child care and training, and . . . child care and training should be separated, carried out by different people according to different styles. Let me try to clarify my use of the terms *education, child care,* and *training.* My argument will make very little sense unless the reader keeps in mind that what I mean by education is *not* development but the *effort to influence* development. Schools cannot cease to be places where an effort is made to direct or shape these processes. That is what I mean by schools dropping their educational function.

Child care is distinguished from education by its relative neutrality. It consists of providing resources, services, activities, love, and attention for children, but with no attempt to influence the course of their development. When the baby-sitter decides that the parents are not doing a good job of bringing up their child and she begins trying to sneak in a little influence of her own, she is no longer limiting herself to child care: she is starting to educate. Parents typically educate, and it is my contention . . . that they are the only ones who have a clear-cut right to educate. They know how they want their child to turn out, even if only in the most general terms, and they try to make him develop in that way. This is as true of permissive parents as it is of authoritarian ones, although they may differ in their educational goals and how they pursue them.

Training is also directive in its intent. However, its objective is not to produce a certain kind of child, but merely to produce a certain kind of performance in the child. What the child does with his acquired skill, how it is integrated into his personality, is a concern that lies beyond training. It is an educational concern. Therefore, to say that schools should abandon education but continue training children is to say the school should narrow their teaching efforts to a simple concern with getting children to perform adequately in reading, writing, and arithmetic.

Such narrowing of teaching effort is likely to strike school people as immoral. What is to become of the child as a whole? Although I can by no means prove it, I want to show as best I can . . . that schools do not and cannot successfully educate—that is, influence how children turn out in any important way. The most they can do successfully is provide child care and training. They could do a much better job of both than they do now, but in order to be free

30

to do a better job they must abandon the idealistic but misguided effort to educate.

* * * * *

The impossibility of mass education is not at all difficult to explain. The kind of influence that would make a genuine difference in the kinds of people children turn out to be must generally come from a long and close personal relationship of the Socratic, the parent-child, or the Emile-and-his-tutor kind.[1] It isn't reasonable to expect such influence to arise out of the conditions of mass schooling, no matter how that schooling is conducted. Even if the public were willing to support schooling to the extent of paying for one teacher for every ten children (thus nearly tripling present school budgets), it wouldn't work, because it would mean drawing in armies of less capable teachers. The teaching profession is already so large that it can never comprise anything more select than a cross section of the college-educated population.

What we find in the elementary schools now is an idealistic commitment to the *idea* of education on the part of people who were mainly drawn into teaching because of a liking for children—whose actual motivations, in other words, are toward child care. The weight of opinion from all sources compels teachers to think of themselves as educators, for, wherever they turn, child care is spoken of condescendingly and training is usually spoken of with contempt. Yet at the same time the schools are under daily attack for doing a bad job, and it is not for failing to educate but for doing a poor job of child care and training.

What Do You Think? ————————————————————————

1. If schools were designed to omit "education," where then would education (as Bereiter defines it) take place? Who would make the "effort to influence" youngsters?

2. Could any political state be content to leave "education" out of the public schools?

3. What kind of teachers would be needed in the school Bereiter describes?

4. Do you agree with the author's argument? Why or why not?

5. Are most teachers drawn to teaching because of a liking for children? For what other reasons might a person become a teacher?

ACTIVITIES FOR INVOLVEMENT

1. Draw up a list of things that you believe an ideal school system in the United States should emphasize by the year 2000. What major goals

[1]Emile, the subject of a novel by J. J. Rousseau, was "educated" by the absence of teaching, that is, he developed "naturally." See Reading 4 in Chapter 5.

would you have your ideal school try to accomplish? Make a list of such goals and compare it with those of your classmates. See if you can formulate a class list of desired goals for 2000 A.D. (You might find Alvin Toffler's *Learning for Tomorrow: The Role of the Future in Education* (New York: Random House, Inc. 1974) helpful to consult as you plan your educational system.)

2. Hold a panel discussion on the question of appropriate aims for education. Have each member research one of the classic statements of educational aims, e.g., liberal education, education for the needs of the state (See Plato's *Republic*), vocational education, or Perkinson's education for critical skills. Investigate past examples of one of these classic systems. What was the result in practice?

3. Ask your school principal or a guest speaker from a nearby college to discuss the question of educational goals. Ask the speaker in advance to give views on the way in which educational goals do or do not control the details of education in the United States.

4. Conduct a survey among a random sample of fellow students to determine what they believe the school should emphasize. Tally their responses. Then conduct a second survey among a random sample of adults in your community. Tally their responses. Then compare the responses of your two samples. What differences do you notice? Similarities? How would you explain these differences and similarities?

5. Write a brief paper in which you argue for or against the topic, "Resolved: Any effective system of education must include students in the planning of educational goals."

6. Listed below are a number of statements urging a particular emphasis for the schools:
    (a) Schools should teach students "to think."
    (b) Schools should develop good citizens.
    (c) Schools should prepare individuals for the world of work.
    (d) Schools should assist individuals to adjust to the particular communities in which they live.
    (e) Schools should promote a greater sense of self-awareness.
    (f) Schools should develop individuals dedicated to bringing about change in their society.
    Rank these in order from most to least important. Would you add any statements to the list? Delete any? Is there any combination of statements that you would argue for? Be prepared to defend your choice.

7. The charts (p. 33) suggest in a compelling way how education contributes to economic well-being. Suppose someone wanted to argue *against* these figures. What sorts of arguments could he use? How valid would such arguments be?

With More Schooling—How Yearly Income Climbs

Average annual income for males

Age Group	Level of Education Completed			
	Grade School	High School	College 4 Years	College 5 Years or More
25–34	$7,755	$10,859	$13,274	$14,859
35–44	$9,776	$12,997	$20,085	$22,603
45–54	$9,693	$13,528	$22,307	$24,239
55–64	$8,873	$12,624	$19,765	$24,525
65 and over	$5,174	$7,768	$12,677	$15,013

Note: Figures based on official data for 1972 average income, adjusted to reflect April, 1974, consumer prices.
Basic data: U.S. Census Bureau: 1974 adjustment by USN&WR Economic Unit

A Lifetime's Earnings—The Impact of Education

Estimated total income from age 18 to death for males with varying levels of education—

Less than 8 years	$280,000
Grade school completed	$345,000
High school—1 to 3 years	$390,000
High school completed	$480,000
College—1 to 3 years	$545,000
College completed	$710,000
College—5 years or more	$825,000

Note: Earnings are in 1972 dollars.
Source: U.S. Census Bureau

Reprinted from *U.S. News & World Report*, July 22, 1974. Copyright 1974 U.S. News & World Report, Inc.

33

4
HOW GOOD ARE
THE SCHOOLS?

The public schools are under attack these days from many quarters. How well do they educate the youngsters that confront them every year? Do the schools perform as well as they should? How well should they perform? This chapter presents several impressions of how well the schools are doing.

1. What J.H.S. 45 on 120th Street and First Avenue Is Like*

Many people are not aware of what it is really like inside some inner-city classrooms. In this reading, a beginning teacher writes the Dean of her School of Education to describe what she found in her first teaching assignment.

Dear Dean Sizer:

You probably will not remember me as we met only briefly. I was a candidate for a Master of Arts in teaching last year. Now I am teaching in a junior high school in Spanish Harlem; and my experiences last year and this prompt me to communicate some of my criticisms. Although a good deal of the time I feel the faults lie on my own shoulders, there might be something useful in what's to follow. . . .

How to tell you about JHS 45 on 120th St. and First Ave.?

At 8:40 I am meant to be standing in the hall outside my classroom, welcoming in my children, preventing them from running down the halls, killing each other, passing cigarettes, etc.; however, I can't make it to the hall because I haven't mastered the taking of the attendance yet. Each day I have four separate attendance sheets to fill out (twice, needs to be done after lunch). A criss and then a cross in blue or black ink. Red pen for mistakes. About eight different kinds of notations for different sorts of lateness. Postcards home, right then, for those who are absent. "T-slip" for probation for those who are absent five days. At the end of each week there's the fifth attendance form, which involves averages.

*Excerpted from Amy Kovner, "A Plea From The Ghetto," *American Education,* December 1966—January 1967.

Gerald Glass comes bopping in, no longer screaming obscenities with each breath . . . ; he leans over my desk and for the third time this week there's liquor on his early-morning breath. "Why, Gerald, you know school isn't the place to come in drunk to." "Kovnah, I ain't drunk. I know how to hold my liquor." What to say?

Three minutes to get Juan to sit down; two minutes to get Raul to take off his jacket. Raul is my favorite boy, but I think he's gone to prison school upstate for some little indiscretion he committed during Christmas. Raul hit me hard one day, but I like him so. Somebody passing down the hall throws an egg at Louise; Christine refuses to be seated because on her chair is a large obscene drawing. Everywhere there is obscene poetry; a festival of bubble gum, candy wrappers, spitballs, stolen pens, inveterate boredom, carelessness, profound illiteracy.

The whole place is mad and absurd; going to school is going to war. My classes are devoted to trying to get the kids to open their notebooks, stay seated, stop talking, stop fighting, stop exhibiting themselves, stop writing obscenities in the text, stop asking to go to the bathroom, stop blowing bubbles, stop, stop, stop. We have not started to *learn* yet, I am afraid. When I admit this to my colleagues, they retort, "Miss Kovner, you must learn to keep your classroom door closed when you're having trouble." . . . Whether I'll be able to last out more than a year at 45 (which is more to the point), I don't know.

Yours,
Amy Kovner

What Do You Think? _____

1. Miss Kovner implies that "slum" teachers have a war on their hands. Many teachers in the affluent suburbs also find their positions unpleasant and many students hostile. Why might this be so?
2. Some of the problems described in the article are extreme, such as the drinking problem with Gerald. Should teachers have to put up with such difficult situations? What can be done about it?
3. What would you do if you were Miss Kovner?

2. A Black Parent Speaks*

Many parents of minority group children believe that the schooling their children receive is inappropriate to their needs. Here one father expresses his concern:

*Excerpted from "We Have Marched, We Have Cried, We Have Prayed," Ebony, April 1968.

You know what you're going to tell your kid? George Washington, Patrick Henry, the great patriots—Benjamin Franklin discovered that lightning and electricity are synonymous. Everybody who ever did anything is white.

Here is what you are going to give my child. I am going to send him to school and teach him to respect authority. So here is a cracker teacher standing in front of my child making him listen to *Little Black Sambo*. See, that's the image the school gives him when he's young to teach him his "place." A caricature, wearing outlandish clothing that even the animals in the forest don't want to wear. His name is "Sambo." His mother's name is "Mumbo." And his father's name is "Jumbo." What are you telling him about family ties in America? That child does not have the same last name as either one of his parents. Since his parents have different last names, they are not even married.

All right. So he goes through the caricature like I did when I was a small child in grade school. And I don't forget these things. I wasn't born from the womb with the attitudes I have now. They were put in me by crackers. I sat through *Little Black Sambo*. And since I was the only black face in the room, I became Little Black Sambo. If my parents had taught me bad names to call the little cracker kids—and I use that term on purpose to try to get a message across to you—you don't like it. Well, how do you think we feel when an adult is going to take our child (we teach our child to respect that adult) and that adult gives these little white kids bad names to call him? Why don't you have Little Cracker Bohunk? Little Cracker Dago? Little Cracker Kike? You can't stand that. But yet you're going to take our little black children and expose them to this kind of ridicule, then not understand why we don't like it.

All right. After he is Nigger Jim, he goes to high school and reads *Emperor Jones* written by Eugene O'Neill, who they are taught is a great playwright. And not only do they have to read it silently and master it, they've got to come to school and discuss orally about the "bush niggers." But still nothing about kikes. And nothing about dagos and spiks and wetbacks and bohunks and wops.

And then after he has passed through these degrading ages of the black man, and they have whipped the spirit out of him—after they have made him feel he's not fit to walk the earth and he always has to apologize to you for being here, then they crown him. They say, "I'm going to tell you what your grand-daddy had been; what your daddy had been; what you are going to be: Old Black Joe. And you know how Old Black Joe comes? With his head hanging low.

You tell us what you want to do to us and make of us. And this is the "educational process" which our children go through. And you wonder why they don't want to sit up in school.

What Do You Think?

Suppose you were a teacher or principal. What would you say to this parent?

3. Public Education Is in Serious Trouble

Next, three short readings, each of which presents a rather grim picture of public education. Can such conditions be remedied?

A. Education—Too Little, Too Late*

Public education in this country is in trouble—serious trouble—particularly in the nation's major cities.

In his speech several weeks ago to the South Carolina Education Association in Columbia, James A. Harris, newly elected president of the National Education Association, told it like it is, painting a stark, grim, threatening education picture with these facts:

- There are nearly 2 million school-aged children who are not in school. Most of them live in large cities.
- Of the students who are attending classes, more of them will spend some portion of their lives in a correctional institution than those who will attend all of the institutions of higher learning.
- Take any school day of the year, and you will find 13,000 kids of school age in correctional institutions and another 100,000 in jail or police lockups.
- Of every 100 students attending school across the nation, 23 drop out, 77 graduate from high school, 43 enter college, 21 receive a B.A., 6 earn an M.A., and 1 earns a Ph.D.
- Crime and violence in central city schools are growing at unprecedented rates. In the higher schools of some cities there are literally thousands of students who have no interest in education, who roam the corridors, disrupt the classes, constantly look for trouble or foment it.

Four years ago Henry T. Hillson, president of the New York City High School Principals Association, said of this group: "Unless the Board of Education and the state Legislature take action with respect to some kind of control or some kind of special schooling for this disruptive group, within a limited period of years we won't have a good academic high school left in the city. And that goes for every big city where there is a population problem."

Many states now spend more money to incarcerate[1] a child than to provide him with an education. In Iowa, for example, the state will pay $9,000 a year to maintain a student in the juvenile home at Eldora but only $1,050 a year for an ordinary student who behaves himself.

*From "Education—Too Little, Too Late," *Parade,* June 16, 1974.
[1]Lock up.

Maryland spends $1,800; Illinois and Michigan $10,000; Virginia $3,877, and the District of Columbia $7,469 per child for one year in a correctional institution, far less on the average student who needs no correction.

What is necessary, he says, is for the Federal Government to increase its share of the education dollar.

"We need 670,000 additional teachers to upgrade educational programs," [Harris] asserts. "Four hundred thousand are needed to reduce class sizes, 245,000 are needed for special programs, 21,000 are needed for kindergarten, and 6,000 to reinstate programs cut."

Harris feels strongly that education should be pushed to the top of the nation's priority list. Many citizens who year after year keep voting down various school bond issues apparently do not.

B. Crime Within the School*

The Sixth Annual Gallup Poll of Public Attitudes Toward Education expressed a concern that a growing problem within the school is crime. The following two questions were added to the survey in 1974:

The first question asked:

From what you have heard or read, is it your impression that stealing (money, clothes, lunches, books, etc.) goes on a great deal, some, or very little in the local public schools?

The second question asked:

Are student gangs that disrupt the school or bother other students a big problem, somewhat of a problem, or not a problem in the local public schools

	National Totals %	No Children In Schools %	Public School Parents %	Parochial School Parents %	High School Juniors & Seniors %
Stealing					
Goes on a great deal	33	30	35	50	37
Some	34	31	39	29	47
Very little	15	13	18	5	15
Don't know/no answer	18	26	8	16	1
Student Gangs					
Yes, a big problem	17	18	14	21	14
Somewhat of a problem	31	29	33	36	40
Not a problem	32	26	44	28	45
Don't know/no answer	20	27	9	15	1

*Dr. George H. Gallup, *Phi Delta Kappan,* September 1974, p. 21.

The findings are disturbing, and suggest that something must be done if the public's confidence and respect for the school is to remain at a high level. Critics will almost certainly point to the schools as a breeding ground for crime and violence and for future Watergates.[2]

Analysis of the finding by areas of the nation and by size of city sheds further light on the problem of crime within the schools.

The question

From what you have heard or read, is it your impression that stealing (money, clothes, lunches, books, etc.) goes on a great deal, some, or very little in the local *public* schools?

	Great Deal %	Some %	Very Little %	Don't Know/ No Answer %
National	33	34	15	18
Sex				
Men	29	35	17	19
Women	36	34	12	18
Race				
White	32	36	14	18
Nonwhite	35	26	21	18

C. The Anatomy of a School Vandal*

The window-breaker, the fixture smasher, the paint splatterer—how do we account for his actions? He's a student dissatisfied with his education, and [he] takes out his unhappiness on the school. Maybe.

Sociologists who have looked deeply into the problem find other reasons. They suggest that the vandal may be one of these:

• The vindictive, who carries a grudge against a particular teacher or other staff member.
• The malicious, who commits his acts out of sheer deviltry.
• The ideological, who wishes to dramatize some particular stance or cause.
• The acquisitive, who combines destruction with theft.
• The bored, who has few constructive outlets for his energies.
• The frustrated, who, for one reason or another, sees the easily accessible neighborhood school as a symbol of a society which he believes is cal-

[2]Refers to the Watergate complex, where Democratic Party headquarters were broken into in 1972, resulting eventually in criminal charges against many in the administration and in the resignation of President Nixon.

*Reprinted, with permission, from *The American School Board Journal,* January 1972. Copyright 1972, the National School Boards Association. All rights reserved.

lously indifferent to his needs and aspirations and against which he can express all his rage and impotence through school vandalism.

The school vandal is a student between the ages of eight and fourteen, surveys by public school officials have discovered. The F.B.I. says he's more likely to be in the 12-to-14-years age bracket. An F.B.I. crime report states that of 100,000 recent arrests for vandalism, 77 percent of the vandals were under 18 years of age and the largest number was from 12 to 14 years of age.

... AND HOW ONE DISTRICT CATCHES HIM

The District of Columbia school system installed a noise detection system which in three months led directly to the apprehension and arrest of 22 persons. The system is believed to be the main reason vandalism losses dropped to $13,000 for December 1970—down from $19,720 for December 1969.

It works like this:

The schools are electronically linked to a console located in the city's municipal center. When a door or window in one of the schools is opened after hours, an electric circuit is completed, and a light and buzzer are activated next to the school's name on the console (which is watched round-the-clock). An operator then switches on the school's public address system which becomes a sensitive electronic "ear" that enables the operator to listen in at the school. If something sounds suspicious, the operator calls the police.

What Do You Think? _____

1. How do you explain the frequency in both urban and suburban schools of damaging attacks by vandals?

2. Find out what your school district spent on repairing the damage done by vandals last year. Then draw up a budget for the needed things that could have been purchased with the lost money.

3. What can students, or student government, do to cut down on vandalism?

4. Some educators argue that the decision in many communities not to spend more money on public education is shortsighted, in that it will cost each of us far more money in the long run. Would you agree? Why or why not?

5. Would these national findings in the polls on pp. 39–40 be reflected in your own school setting? Take a similar poll in your own community and find out.

---

4. Guns in the Schools?*

What sorts of conditions in schools would require administrators to carry guns? Read on—and find out!

*"A Mixed Reaction in Alabama to Teachers Who Carry Guns," *Washington Post* in *Sunday Punch,* San Francisco *Examiner & Chronicle,* March 3, 1974.

One day last spring, Billy Thomas Marsh, the principal of Phillips high school, was performing one of those unpleasant non-educational chores which occasionally plague school administrators.

A group of intruders wandered in off the streets, roamed the corridors for a while, and became belligerent when Marsh and his aides tried to move them outside.

"One of them doubled back through a side door," Marsh recalls, "and there I was looking into the barrel of a .38." Marsh hit the floor as a bullet crashed into a nearby water cooler.

Recounting the confrontation these days, Marsh fingers the flattened slug which he has carried in his pocket ever since as a reminder.

"We decided right then that if the outsiders were going to play that way, we would too," he said in a cheerful, unemotional voice. He began taking his own .32-caliber revolver to school.

His wasn't an unprecedented reaction. Ensley high school principal Robert Lee Lott's life was threatened several times after he had a student arrested for pushing dope. So he started carrying his Smith and Wesson .38-caliber pistol to school in his briefcase.

Another principal routinely took his pistol to work and locked it in his car trunk during school hours. A student adviser at Phillips high carried a .22-caliber revolver in a belt holster just before school holidays.

These and other similar revelations startled Birmingham, raising the question of whether there is any justification for administrators or teachers having guns in the schools.

An investigation by superintendent Wilmer S. Cody found 13 principals, advisers and teachers who either routinely or occasionally had carried weapons. On January 22, the Board of Education banned all lethal weapons from school grounds unless Cody specifically authorizes them.

"I've never heard of a case where the staffs [of schools] were armed," says William Henry, an official of the American Association of School Administrators.

Cody queried 50 big-city school systems and discovered most don't have any gun-toting policy. Exceptions were Atlanta and Norfolk, which authorize certain officials to be armed.

"It worried me because it raises the question of whether you can have people carrying guns who can't handle a conflict situation," says Cody, who has been superintendent here since October. "I'm worried that we might have someone out of naivete or ignorance using a gun in school."

It was just such a hazardous mishap that prompted disclosure of the pistol-packing principals. A month ago, Alfred N. Green, boys' adviser at Ensley high, was having an argument over discipline with a student in his office. The youth became angry and barged behind Green's desk to get at the telephone.

Green, who said he was pushed hard against a wall, told officials he opened his desk drawer and took out his gun. He said he merely was showing it as a warning. The student claimed Green pointed it at him.

Ensley principal Lott, who is Green's boss, says he wishes "the incident hadn't happened" and wishes that neither he nor Green had to have guns at the school. But it had seemed the best way to prepare for unwanted trouble after his experience with the school dope-peddler.

It was last spring and, after twice disciplining the boy, Lott had him arrested. Shortly afterward, he began receiving threatening telephone calls from a young man believed to be a nonstudent friend of the arrested youth. It was then that Lott and Green both began bringing pistols.

Neither Lott nor any of the others raised the question of hiring security guards because they believed the incidents were too infrequent and they don't like the idea of uniformed men patrolling school corridors. They preferred to handle the cases themselves.

Public reaction has been mixed. There were very few indignant outbursts. Considerable sympathy for the plight of the principals has been expressed. "There has been a curious absence of public furor," says superintendent Cody, who has had only four phone calls on the subject.

A sampling of students registered unequivocal approval of their principals. "I can understand why they carry guns," declares Rodney Pullum, 17, a Phillips senior. "You've got some kids from outside who are always coming here to raise trouble."

What Do You Think? _____

1. Should school administrators be armed? What about teachers?
2. Can schools be made safe enough so that administrators will not need guns? If so, how?

5. What Students Think about Schools*

How do kids feel about schools? The reading which follows gets at the feelings of students in San Francisco, California. You may be surprised at what you read.

Send your kid to a San Francisco public school and if he doesn't come hobbling home some day, bloodied in a schoolyard stabbing, chances are he'll wind up nodding out on junk. At best, let him go to a school in the City and you condemn him to weekend karate classes so he can hold his own in fights, headaches and nervous tics from the ever-present racial tension, and a chaotic classroom environment where even a genius couldn't learn.

*Robert Kanigel, "Our City Schools: What the Kids Think," *San Francisco Magazine,* January 1974. Reprinted by permission. To appear in somewhat different form in *City Sunrise* by Robert Kanigel.

This is the kind of lop-sided view of city schools that makes so many Americans reject the city as a place to raise their children. According to a national survey commissioned by U.S. Home Corporation, 71 percent of families leaving cities for the suburbs cited better schools for their children as an "absolutely essential" factor in their decisions.

As a whole, city kids *do* score lower on standardized reading and math tests, statistics show. And the papers *do* seem to report more trouble in city schools—more fights, narcotics use, racial incidents. But whatever its failings, the city school offers an extra dimension one in suburbia can't match—the drama and diversity of the city itself. "The most extensive facility imaginable for learning is our urban environment," writes Richard Saul Wurman, editor of *Yellow Pages of Learning Resources.* "It is a classroom without walls . . . offering a boundless curriculum with unlimited expertise." And many local students who have gone to suburban schools before moving to San Francisco feel the same way about it.

Talk to Tad Gilman (all student's names have been changed), a Lincoln High School senior who attended first through tenth grades in suburban Sacramento schools: "Living in the City I think you learn more about the world, and how to get along. In the suburbs you don't experience anything else; everybody's white, looks the same, dresses the same. But here, you open your eyes and you get a chance to see all those different races and ethnic groups and life styles." Of every hundred of Tad's Lincoln High classmates, more than forty come from minority groups.

In 1971, there was trouble at Lincoln—and plenty of front-page newspaper coverage publicizing it. Racial fights, muggings and extortions seemed to be the daily fare. Enrolling near the height of all the commotion was Tad Gilman. At first, he recalls, "I was sort of uneasy. I didn't know how to handle myself." But he soon learned "that if you played it right you could avoid all the violence you kept hearing about. . . . In all the time I've been here, I've never been in a fight. I've never gotten hit over the head. I've never gotten jumped. If you ask me, the people who end up getting hurt are the same people who start the trouble in the first place."

Tad, a quiet, light-haired 18-year-old whose father is a telephone company executive, sums up his two years at Lincoln this way: "It was an experience," he says with a hint of a grin. "I think everybody should do it." Not that he overly loves the City; on the contrary, Tad, who trains birds as part of a City Zoo-sponsored program, prefers the country, even the suburbs. "I wouldn't want my kids to grow up in the City all their lives. But I would want them to experience it, maybe live in the City a couple of years so they'd know what it was like."

Whatever students like Tad Gilman actually learn in class, the stimulation, even the conflict they're exposed to in a City school like Lincoln can itself prove educational. Author Alvin Toffler argues in *Future Shock,* for example, that in a world gone crazy with change, learning to handle stress and stimulus can be as important as mastering specific knowledge and skills. But most parents, safe to say, don't hold so broad a view of education. And spurred by the public furor over the issue of busing, many of them—including some ordinarily classed as "liberal"—have come to question whether racially and ethnically mixed schooling is really worth all the fuss.

Many of their doubts were spoken to in a 1972 federally sponsored study covering the first year of busing in San Francisco. One of its most significant findings concerned the degree to which students viewed their own race as better or more important than others—"ethnocentrism" in the researchers' jargon. The sixth-graders studied showed a 14 percent drop in ethnocentrism in busing's first year.

Academically, the integrated school system hadn't improved much; reading, arithmetic and social studies scores were still below national averages, the study reported. However, it expressed optimism with the consistent finding that Richmond District pupils, who'd been integrated for two years instead of one, scored higher than the rest of the City, in some cases exceeding national norms. Best news of all was that Richmond District 6th graders, instead of lagging behind the nation as did the rest of the District, had made reading gains at a "month-for-month" clip.

A most unexpected study finding was that *parents* of bused children seemed more pleased with the busing program than those whose children were not bused; for instance, only 49 percent of parents of non-bused children reported few or no problems in the area of child safety, compared to 79 percent of parents of bused children. Busing was more to be feared in the abstract, as a symbol, than as everyday reality.

Not that it was no longer the butt of bitter attacks—it still was. But significantly, by the end of the first year, almost seven out of ten parents of bused children were willing to give the program passing grades ("satisfactory" or better). Moreover, one of the consequences most feared of busing—that bused kids would have more trouble making friends—proved unfounded; fewer parents damned busing for their children's "difficulty making friends" (18 percent) than praised it for "increased cultural knowledge" and "developing friendships" (30 percent and 39 percent).

Drawing students from a far wider area than do elementary schools, City secondary schools are often "naturally" integrated. San Francisco's Roosevelt Junior High, for example, with its 33 percent white, 29 percent black, 24 percent Chinese, 4 percent Spanish-speaking, 4 percent Japanese and 3 percent Filipino enrollment, mirrors well the City-wide breakdown of minority students. Roosevelt draws blacks from the nearby Fillmore District ghetto, Chinese, whites and some blacks from the Inner Richmond, more whites from the Presidio military reservation. And it's these kids from Army families, perhaps, kids who never before attended anything but suburban or rural schools, who might best be able to tell us what going to a San Francisco school is like. What about those fights and stabbings? What about those racial tensions? What about the ever-present drugs?

Billy Buchanan, a 7th-grader whose Army father is an instructor on the Presidio, reports that people just aren't as friendly in the City as in his native Idaho. "Here you have to watch out more," he says. "The kids deliberately knock you over. They think it's a gag. And sometimes, in class, you can't do your work because some of the colored kids are up and stomping around." **45**

Billy fits neatly the stereotype of the funny-looking, well-mannered kid who goes around saying "yes" instead of "yeah," wears heavy, black-framed glasses that are too big for his wispy, blond-haired head and generally comes across as a pushover. Appropriately, Billy's guidance counselor calls him "immature for age—an easy prey." Poor Billy would have his problems almost anywhere away from the quiet, unthreatening atmosphere of the small town in Idaho in which he was brought up and went to school. Back in Idaho, Billy remembers, "Everybody knew everybody. Everybody smiled. Nobody cussed that much." His school sat in the middle of a big field. "Just a plain, little old school," he calls it, where there were "no colored people, no Chinese people, no nothing. About the only kind of people we had were people who maybe had a little Scotch blood in them."

But even for a boy as plainly unsuited to city life as Billy, the City has some redeeming qualities. "San Francisco is so exciting," says Billy, "so many places to go and everything." He's learned a lot, too—including a kind of first lesson in human relations: "You have to move aside sometimes [in the hallways], because sometimes the other kids just *won't.*"

Roosevelt students like Billy who previously attended small town or suburban schools all agree that in the City they have to be more alert to the chance that a sticky situation will flare up into a fight; but unlike Billy, most of them seem to take that fact of life comfortably in stride. Ken Doyle, for example, a likeable 12-year-old originally from Stamford, Connecticut, notes that even if he does get into a tangle now and again, "It's just the kids fooling around. I don't get hurt or anything." He says he misses the big suburban plot his parents had in Connecticut where you could throw a Frisbee around. But back there, too, "you had to go all the way downtown just to see a movie and when you got there, there just wasn't that much there."

A pretty 9th-grader who most recently went to school in Garden Grove, in Orange County, Sue Miller, says that suburban kids are "quieter" than city kids because "in the suburbs it's real peaceful and there's not much happening." Of the suburbs, she adds: "I like it to be quiet, but I don't like it to be boring."

Andy Starr, a reflective soft-spoken boy, is the son of a missionary who's in San Francisco for a year of special training before heading overseas. From Sanger, California, a small town a few miles outside Fresno, Andy had been worried about coming to the City. "I thought it would be a real tough school and I'd have a rough time getting along," he says. "But it turned out I was wrong. I haven't had any problems. . . . Of course you have to take it easy for a while, not push too hard; but that's what you'd do for *any* new school."

In the four months he's been at Roosevelt, says Andy, he's never once been offered drugs. Other Roosevelt students say the same—that the spectre of epidemic drug use in City schools is, at the junior high level at least, overblown. Some part of this pretty picture can be ascribed to a natural reluctance to confide in an outsider; and yet some of the kids are quite explicit: "I saw marijuana once when I was in Novato," says one 9th-grader from that San Francisco suburb. "Here I haven't seen it at all." Says Sue Miller, the former Garden Grove suburbanite, after a year at rough, tough Roosevelt: "I've never seen one. I've never seen a junkie in all my life."

For most Roosevelt students who once went to rural and suburban schools, the City is neither some kind of adolescent's paradise nor a hell-hole of vice and violence. Talking about living and going to school in the City, most of the kids just sit back and tell you matter-of-factly what they like and what they don't about the City and their former suburbs. Many conclude that, on balance, they like one or the other better; but a good many say it just doesn't make much difference to them. A taking-it-all-in-stride attitude is the dominant feeling you're left with. The kids call the City "different" or "unusual" —more or less neutral terms; but the kind of antipathy and estrangement so many Americans feel toward the city is wholly absent. It's as if the normal, everyday problems they have just being kids makes going to school in a city at worst a secondary trauma.

None of this is to say that San Francisco schools don't have serious problems—they surely do. City schools *do* form the backdrops for not-infrequent fights; they *are* struck, from time to time, by gun and knife incidents. And perhaps more serious than the violence, it *is* true that some students attend City schools for ten or twelve years and at the end simply can't put together a clear, grammatical English sentence.

But such failings are not so much those of City schools *per se* as they are of society as a whole; for the kids most alienated from the earnest and orderly classroom environment our society deems the norm and ideal, come mostly **47** from just those minority families least able to derive a measure of security and dignity through "The System." Serving as San Francisco stomping grounds for many such minority kids—especially the Chicanos of the surrounding Mission District *barrio,* but many blacks and Filipinos as well—Mission High School manifests most of the conditions associated with "inner city" schools.

Absenteeism at once overshadows and aggravates the school's other problems. Of some 2600 Mission students, around 750 stay home on a typical day. Mission teachers note that so horrendous an attendance record is not alone due to student alienation from school—though all agree it plays a part. In many poor families where the mother must work, they explain, older children often take on quasi-parental duties and simply don't have *time* for school.

Reading and math ability of Mission students is *very* poor—typically two years behind the rest of the City, three years behind the nation.

Ex-Mission students joke about how tough the school was—but insist that a serious student can come away from Mission with a pretty decent education. And yet, the time and energy its teachers must devote just to keeping track of absent students, working through the language barrier and dealing with students for whom school problems are the least of their worries, can't help but take its toll: Mission simply doesn't have the kind of academically dynamic atmosphere in which a young and vital, intellectually inclined mind can best develop and grow.

But as only one of eight academic high schools in the City, Mission High alone shouldn't form the basis for judging San Francisco schools; no more than should Lowell High, the City's elite academic high school. For while San Francisco high school students as a whole fall a year and more behind in reading and math skills, Lowell kids, sporting an average IQ of 115, routinely come in two years above the nation on most measures of scholastic performance.

Moreover, what is learned from the City itself cannot be put in statistics. Carol Adams is a pretty 17-year-old with brown hair falling lightly to her shoulders in gentle curls. She's a senior at Lincoln High now, but for most of her life she went to school in Evansville, Indiana. Just after she got to San Francisco, she recalls, she was walking along a residential street near school and heard some people on a stoop talking in a strange, foreign tongue— something she wasn't used to back in Indiana. "I was terrified," she remembers. "I thought they were talking about me!"

Carol's come a long way since then and by now has had a chance to put her months in a City school into a little perspective. She doesn't think her teachers, generally, are as good as those she had in Indiana. ("Some of them are old and out of date.") And echoing a complaint made by many ex-suburbanites, she says she finds many of her teachers are too lax in enforcing rules and disciplining students.

But everything considered, says Carol, going to school in the City has had a "good effect on me. Here," she says, "you have to learn to adjust to different people, people who speak different languages. Back in Indiana I didn't have a chance to learn that much about life. Here, somehow, I feel more on my own.

48 It's opened my eyes a lot. I feel freer."

1. According to these students, what seem to be the advantages of going to school in San Francisco? The disadvantages? Would this be true of most large cities?
2. Could you propose any ways to correct the problems discussed?
3. What might smaller, more rural schools do to provide some of the benefits the students interviewed found in attending city schools? Do smaller rural schools have some advantages which large urban schools do not? If so, what might they be?

6. Are High-Schoolers Now Learning Less?*

Over the last ten years, "College Board" examination results have registered a continuous drop. What do the data indicate about American secondary schools?

Concern has risen anew over whether the education being offered in America's elementary and secondary schools is satisfactory.

A fresh round of debate erupted in mid-December after average scores were announced for "College Board" examinations given to high-school seniors last spring by the Educational Testing Service, of Princeton, N.J.

These examinations, taken by students intending to go on to college, showed this when compared with prior results:

There was a slight drop in scores from the previous year in mathematical testing and a much larger decline in ratings on the verbal test.

Over a decade, test scores have registered a virtually continuous decrease —adding up to a fall-off of 35 points in scores on verbal tests and 21 points in results on mathematics. This represents a drop of 13 per cent and 7 per cent, respectively, based on a lowest possible score of 200 points.

To some educators, last spring's outcome reinforced long-held doubts about the kind of education American youngsters are getting below college level.

Some put the blame on what they termed deficiencies going back to early grades of elementary school—confronting high schools with the job of doing far too much remedial work on inadequately prepared students.

Others, such as Dr. B. Frank Brown, chairman of the National Commission on the Reform of Secondary Education, saw the results as an indictment of high schools themselves. Said Dr. Brown, himself a former high-school principal:

"It's one more indication that high schools are in a state of extreme intellectual disrepair.

*"Are High-Schoolers Now Learning Less?" *U.S. News & World Report,* December 31, 1973. Copyright 1973 U.S. News & World Report, Inc.

"I thought it was me, but maybe the school's no damn good."

Drawing by Charles Addams; © 1974 The New Yorker Magazine, Inc.

"At least half of the teaching in secondary schools today is devoted in one way or another to social relationships, and this is watering down the curriculum. The farther we get from the more rigorous academic courses in English, math and science, the more these scores are going to decline."

On the opposing side were educators who contended that testing for admission to college was not an adequate measure of the over-all quality of education now being provided in U.S. elementary and secondary schools.

These professionals said that such tests 10 years ago were administered largely to top-notch students aiming for admission to one of the highly selective institutions which required the tests.

Today, the educators pointed out, less-selective colleges and universities also require applicants to take the tests—with the result that less able students are having more impact on scores.

These educators also cited the growing tendency of colleges to accept high scores made by the best students in the junior year of high school. Averages on senior-year tests, therefore, include proportionately more low scores made by the "slower" students who needed a second try at the tests.

Robert J. Solomon, executive vice president of the Educational Testing Service, added a defense of educational quality in elementary and secondary schools.

In a virtually identical "warm up" examination given to all potential candidates for college early in the 11th grade, he said, scores have remained almost the same over the last 10 years. He described this examination as "a better measure of average ability because the kind of students taking it hasn't changed much over the years."

Even so, critics and defenders of U.S. education agreed that the results pointed up the need for a closer look at what America's young people actually are learning as children and adolescents.

Said Dr. T. Anne Cleary of the College Entrance Examination Board, based in New York City:

"The fact that verbal scores are dropping faster than mathematical scores would point to something outside the schools. It's obvious, for instance, that children are spending more time watching television and less time reading and conversing intelligently."

Also advanced was the possibility that scores might be influenced by the intensifying effort of educators to keep even the poorest students in schools. And some educators wondered if traditional tests were adequately measuring the learning acquired through new teaching methods and the electronic media.

Needed, these educators said, is a thorough testing of all students to help evaluate the effectiveness of schools and teachers. Their conclusion: Until such over-all testing is done, doubts about the quality of education in U.S. elementary and secondary schools are likely to continue unresolved.

What Do You Think?

1. Do the data support Dr. Brown's critique of American high schools?

2. Does your school experience support or refute his criticisms?

3. How persuasive do you find Solomon's rebuttal to the negative interpretation put on the test results?

4. Is it "obvious" that "children are spending more time watching television and less time reading and conversing intelligently"? If so, why?

ACTIVITIES FOR INVOLVEMENT

1. Interview officials in your school district to determine the extent of vandalism and the seriousness of the problem. What is the cost of vandalism to the district each year? What areas of the budget could be improved if money lost to vandalism were available?

    Try to construct a program that might be helpful to students who become vandals and to the schools that suffer from them. Be certain to include an awareness of questions regarding the rights of property as well as the civil rights of students and school authorities.

    Some school districts now require identification badges for students. Would that be helpful in your situation? Are there any problems involved in such a suggestion?

2. Could you devise an article like "What Students Think About Schools" for your school. In other words, conduct a series of interviews to determine whether students feel your school environment contributes to their growth and development.

3. Use the question raised in the reading titled "Are High-Schoolers Now Learning Less?" as the basis for a classroom debate. What kind of information has to be considered on each side of the issue?

4. Hold a round-table discussion on what teacher-training can do to prepare people like Miss Kovner (Reading 1) more adequately to teach in inner-city schools. If possible, invite a professor from such an institution and a community worker to speak to the class on this topic. How do their viewpoints compare?

5. What makes an ideal teacher? Listed below are adjectives describing the kind of person various people believe a teacher should be. Pick the four you believe are most important and the four you believe are least important. Then explain why you selected those you did.

Patient	Loving	Good disciplinarian
Kind	Scholarly	Sensitive
Courteous	Talkative	Firm
Intelligent	Fun	Flexible
Aggressive	Humorous	Have a good voice
Warm	"A good guy"	Attractive
Anxious	Mysterious	Young
Strong-willed	Inspirational	"Take no back talk"

6. Write a brief paper in which you attempt to refute the argument: "There *is* nothing good about education today."

5
WHO SHOULD RUN THE SCHOOLS?

Board of Education Meeting.

Numerous interest groups compete for power in school districts in American cities and suburbs. Local boards of education are often attacked as unresponsive to the people's needs. Parent organizations form to prevent the expansion of the school curriculum into areas such as family life and sex education. Both black and white parents press demands for educational programs each judges necessary for their children.

Long the silent servants of their communities, teachers appear on picket lines demanding a stronger voice in the operation of the schools. Students, encouraged by the lowering of the voting age and the opportunity to enter into school board politics, increasingly seek power. Others, including some members of each of the groups mentioned above, resist any change in control whatsoever, preferring, for a variety of reasons, the status quo.

As you read the selections included in this chapter, try to place your own school district in perspective. What problems does it face? How is it governed? Who has power? Who is seeking it?

1. Should the Superintendent Be In Charge?*

In a blunt interview, the former Superintendent of Schools of Philadelphia discusses why he was asked to resign from one of the largest school systems in the United States. To what extent was politics a factor?

You'd have a tough time convincing Philadelphia's recently ousted superintendent, Mark Shedd, that politics isn't dirty business. Shedd found out firsthand when he became a fiery issue in Police Commissioner Frank Rizzo's campaign for mayor. Rizzo won the job—and Shedd lost his.

Actually, being on the hot seat wasn't new to Shedd. From the moment he was hired five years ago to reform Philadelphia's schools, he became controversial. Most people were either strongly for or strongly against him.

While Shedd's supporters credited him with decentralizing the city's massive school system, streamlining budget management, recruiting top staff, introducing innovative learning programs, and establishing good rapport with students and parents, his detractors claimed otherwise. They said he coddled students, alienated the Philadelphia teachers union by advancing black administrators over whites, and contributed to racial tension by giving in to demands of black students. Sharing this opinion, of course, was Frank Rizzo.

While campaigning for mayor, Rizzo promised to get rid of Shedd. When elected, he appointed three new school board members who tipped the board's balance of power against Shedd. The board quickly demanded—and received—the superintendent's resignation.

*"It's a No-Win Game: An Interview with Mark Shedd," from *Nation's Schools,* LXXIX, March 1972, pp. 66–68.

What is Shedd's reaction to his ouster? Has he gained any insight he'd like to share with other superintendents? Here's what he told *Nation's Schools:*

Q: *Dr. Shedd, what can the typical school administrator learn from your experience in Philadelphia?*

A: When any superintendent takes office, he has to make a judgment concerning the needs of the system and his own style. He has to decide whether he's going to be a caretaker or a change agent. If he chooses the latter, as I did, he has to do so with the foreknowledge that his actions and decisions may make him expendable after about five years. He must be ready to move on after that.

A: *What changes did you attempt to make that put you on the spot?*

A: Probably the most dramatic one was to make the school system more responsive to the needs and concerns of its majority black students. That inevitably meant running counter to the will of the majority of the electorate in the city, the power groups, and the white ethnic groups. For example, take the oft-cited incident in the first two months of my administration—the November 17, 1967, student demonstration before the administration building. In my opinion, it was extremely important and symbolic for the leadership of a major youth-serving institution, the Philadelphia schools, to say, "We're at least willing to listen and to deal with the concerns and demands of black students." But, in the larger political sense, it was suicide.[1]

Let me give you one other illustration. The vast majority of all-black schools had practically no black counselors or administrators. To respond to student needs, assuring that blacks would have people in positions of power to whom they could relate, it was absolutely necessary to create new administrative and counseling positions and to fill them for the most part with blacks. This was done, but only by circumventing traditional civil service procedures for personnel appointments. Though they were priority or exception kinds of appointments, they incurred the ire[2] and the antagonism and the alienation of whites already on the eligibility lists. This action, too, was political suicide in a sense.

Q: *What do you think Mayor Frank Rizzo really meant when, during his campaign, he called you too permissive and threatened to fire you for it?*

A: It goes back to that November 1967 incident when the course of action I followed was diametrically opposed to the course that suited his interests. Police Chief Rizzo personally led the 200 to 300 policemen who charged against the black students demonstrating at the school administration building that day. Even though any untoward student incidents were very rare, he still moved in on the whole group. In my judgment, that was a serious mistake. I chose to meet with the demonstration's leaders, I let them present their

[1]On November 17, 1967, black students demonstrated at the school headquarters over their demands to wear African clothing and haircuts and to have black studies courses. When things appeared to get out of hand, newly sworn-in Police Commissioner Rizzo sent in police. Rizzo partisans called Superintendent Shedd soft and a "molly-coddle." Shedd backers characterized the affair as a near "police riot."

[2]Anger.

demands, and I tried to respond to those demands in a reasonable way. From that day on, Rizzo and I were sworn enemies philosophically.

Q: *Was the 1967 student demonstration incident the only reason Mayor Rizzo was out for your scalp?*

A: No. He was also violently opposed to the student bill of rights and responsibilities which I advocated and which was adopted by the board. It was his feeling, a feeling shared by the Philadelphia Federation of Teachers and a large number of people in the community, that young people are to do what they're told and ask no questions. It's my belief that if students have grievances, there should be a legitimate means of resolving them, short of confrontation. In effect, that's what the student bill of rights and responsibilities did—it set clear limits on student behavior but at the same time provided students with legitimate means of redressing grievances. I think the proof of the pudding is in the eating. Philadelphia hasn't had a major confrontation since the student bill of rights was adopted.

Q: *What part do you feel racial backlash had to play in your forced resignation?*

A: A substantial part. I think there had been a growing resentment, particularly in the predominantly white northeastern part of the city, that more resources, more money, more staffing, and more attention were being given to the inner-city schools, which had the poorest test scores and highest rates of dropouts. Much of the resentment was aimed at me, even though ESEA Title I[3] funds are allocated according to federal policy, not local policy. But the man who's the chief administrator always takes the flak for those things.

Q: *With the benefit of hindsight, is there anything you might have done differently to head off the problems that resulted in your ouster?*

A: Not substantially. You can always go back and say that if you had done this or that differently, some things might have been better. But if I had to choose again whether I would follow the same general strategies that I did as Superintendent, I would. The moves that we made—opening up the system to parents and students; overcoming the administrative inbreeding that had taken place for 40 or 50 years; creating alternatives to existing failing programs, such as the Advancement School, the Parkway program,[4] the West Philadelphia community free school, and the intensive learning center; recruiting people from outside Philadelphia to help run the schools—none of these were popular, but they had to be taken to reverse the consequences of a closed, highly authoritarian, almost regimented, militaristic system.

Q: *Judging from what has happened to you, is there hope for the innovative big-city school administrator?*

A: Hope in what way? That he can take office and hold it indefinitely? No. But if you mean hope that a change-oriented superintendent can move in and

---

[3]Federal funds for improvement of education.
[4]The Parkway program is described in Reading 1 in Chapter 7. It is a highly successful alternative to ordinary school programs.

stay long enough to have an impact, I think that's been demonstrated clearly. We didn't solve all the problems, but the course we followed has been a good one for both the school system and the city. I think many of the less dramatic and more meaningful changes made in the last five years will, eventually, prove themselves, and more and more people will see that things are better now than they were. But it takes 10 to 12 years, a complete school generation, before you really begin to see the benefits of some changes, especially investments in early childhood education and alternative programs.

Q: *Do you believe any of your accomplishments in Philadelphia will be undone by the new school board?*

A: It will take more time to tell. I don't think major priorities set by the outgoing board and administration are going to be changed substantially. Nor do I see alternative programs, like Parkway and the Advancement School, being done away with. But I do see the next three or four years more as a period of consolidation than forward movement for change.

Q: *What do you see as the biggest problem facing your successor?*

A: Money. He's starting out with a $40-million budget deficit. One of the good things about education and the superintendency having been a hot campaign issue in Philadelphia is that now Mayor Rizzo is on the spot to make good on campaign promises to keep schools open for the rest of the year. How he's going to do it I don't know, but he made a commitment to the community, and he has got to hold himself accountable. However much I may disagree with the mayor philosophically, I think his having assumed accountability for the support of the schools is a plus politically for education in Philadelphia.

Q: *Are you suggesting that the politicizing of education is not only inevitable, but good for the big cities?*

A: Inevitable and essential. If the schools are going to have enough political clout to secure needed resources, someone representing them should be at the table when the pie is cut up. The superintendent should be a member of the mayor's cabinet. That way you're also more likely to achieve better integration of services among city agencies and the schools.

Q: *If you had to give your successor, Matt Costanzo, one major piece of advice, what would it be?*

A: Don't take the opposition personally. Try not to let it get under your skin. That's the only way you can keep from having ulcers. Do the best you possibly can day in and day out. Call your shots as you see them. And when you've done that, sleep peacefully. In the last analysis, with most decisions you make, you're damned if you do and damned if you don't. These days it's a no-win game, so you might just as well make up your mind to do what you think is right and let the chips fall where they may.

Q: *Has what's happened in Philadelphia made you discouraged or bitter enough to leave public school administration?*

A: Absolutely not. I'm going to keep my options wide open and consider future employment—in another city superintendency, in state education department work, or wherever it may be—in terms of what the people of any community are ready for next and whether I feel I can make a contribution.   **57**

1. What appear to be the major reasons that Superintendent Shedd was fired?
2. Most school superintendents seem to last about five years before resigning (or being asked to resign). Why do you suppose this is so?
3. "But it takes 10 to 12 years, a complete school generation, before you really begin to see the benefits of some changes, especially investments in early childhood education and alternative programs." If that is true, how can one tell whether a school administrator is leading in the right direction?
4. Superintendent Shedd states that when any superintendent takes office, he has to decide whether he's going to be a caretaker or a change agent. Are these the only alternatives open to a superintendent? What other possibilities might there be?
5. Should the greatest attention (resources, money, staff, etc.) be given to inner-city schools—those which have the poorest test scores and highest drop-out rates? Why or why not?
6. Shedd comments that being a school superintendent these days is a "no-win game." What does he mean? Can this be avoided?

2. Let the Ghetto Run Its Own Schools*

Next, we read about some parents who set up their own school—teachers, building, and all.

The new cry coming out of the ghetto is for the black community to control its public schools. Parents and leaders who have been struggling for 10 years to desegregate school systems, or at least to improve the quality of the education being offered to their children, are no longer willing to plead for the white man's mercy, or to appeal to his nobler instincts. Instead they are demanding the right to take the education of their children into independent hands.

It is a radical departure and one that flies in the face of many old assumptions that white people still harbor about Negroes: How can they do it? Where will their foolishness and irresponsibility lead them next? What do the uneducated black people in our urban slums really think they know about public education? . . .

In one city, at least, the movement has gone past talking and reached concrete embodiment in an exuberant new institution. That city is Boston—the city in which public education in America had its beginnings about 300 years ago. . . .

*Excerpted from Jonathan Kozol, "Let the Ghetto Run Its Own Schools," *Saturday Evening Post,* June 1, 1968. Copyright © 1968 by Jonathan Kozol. Reprinted by permission of Brandt & Brandt.

A group of 12 Negro parents in the Roxbury ghetto . . . refused to accept the idea that the children themselves were inferior. They looked at test results, too, and were fascinated and encouraged by a single interesting piece of evidence. Black children in Roxbury, the largest Negro area of the city, were testing at their proper grade levels during the first year or two of their schooling. It was not until fourth grade that a significant gap became apparent. It was not until the school system had had their children another five or six or seven years that these children gave evidence of being authentically "inferior," educationally "retarded."

Is it our children, asked the parents, or is it the nature of the public schooling?

They felt that they knew the answer and were prepared to prove the point by an act of personal courage. . . . [These] parents announced that a fully staffed, community-run grade school was going to open in September [1966]. It would begin with five classes, kindergarten through the fourth grade, a fifth to be added one year later, a sixth the autumn following. Qualified teachers would be hired out of the Boston system, but only teachers the parents knew and trusted. A building would be purchased. Instruction would be individualized. There would be libraries in all classrooms. Curriculum would be sound but innovative. Consultation and expert assistance would be invited, but in no case was control to be taken outside the black community.

The day after that meeting the parents and a small number of white allies went to work. A board was set up, containing eventually about two dozen members. Of these, three fourths were parents, the rest outsiders. Those from the outside were chosen with calculation. Included were two of the most helpful of the group from Cambridge, two people involved in curriculum development, the superintendent of an outstanding suburban school system, and a young attorney who volunteered to write the documents. By the end of July, several teachers had been hired. Three were white, two Negro. All were offered attractive salaries, although the 12 parents had in fact no bank balance yet. By the end of summer, a black headmistress, a woman with extensive experience, had been hired.

But the greatest single act of sheer bravado was the purchase of a beautiful building costing $40,000. Situated across the street from one of the least popular of the overwhelmingly segregated public schools of Roxbury, the building was spotted one morning by one of the board members, and negotiations for purchase were begun immediately. A century's growth of ivy had covered over its dozens of small windows, but when some of the ivy had been cut away, the parents discovered that they were in possession of one of the most cheerful Georgian period pieces in the area.

The purchase of the building called for the signing of a mortgage, and probably it was at that moment, more than at any other, that the people involved with the New School for Children—as it had come to be known— understood the full dimensions of the kind of risk that they were taking. Six black parents and two white people put their names on a second mortgage, not one among them having at that moment more than $100 in the bank or bureau. **59**

"We've got the teachers, we've got the building," said one. "We've got the desks and chairs. We'll open in September."

In September they did open: 70 children with five teachers. The parents' faith in their ability to raise money proved well-founded. In the 18 months following the opening of the school, a total of close to $200,000 was raised in the white suburbs. Fund raising remains a constant struggle, but the backers have been reliable and generous. Money is short, but contributions keep on coming in, bills somehow get paid, and creditors are not usually kept waiting. The school looks forward to beginning its third year of operation next September. Enrollment is expected to advance beyond 100 pupils, of whom about 35 or 40 will be white, and of whom only about one in seven will be asked to pay the $250 tuition. . . .

Parents' faith in the inherent strengths of their own children seems now in retrospect to have been as well-founded as their confidence that they could raise the money. Pupil achievement, in this most unconventional of schools, has increased even by conventional test standards. Third- and fourth-graders test at or above grade level, and pupil motivation and overall excitement are at a continual high. Curriculum, as promised, is individualized. Classrooms are noisy, messy, alive and fascinating. A class of 15 children is likely to be doing 15 different things at the same moment. Standard texts are not in evidence. Teachers and pupils prefer instead to concoct their own texts and to contrive their own curriculum. A steady emphasis on Negro literature and African history is perhaps the only constant feature in an otherwise unrestricted atmosphere. Problems still develop. Inevitably, some days are unhappy, and some projects and teachers don't work out perfectly. But taken by and large, the image that the school presents is energetic, unschool-like and exciting. Recently teachers from within the Boston system have begun to visit, and their responses have been warm and admiring. "When we get depressed," commented one teacher from the school across the hillside, "we go over to the New School during our lunch hour just to watch things happen and to feel more hopeful." . . .

There is one important criticism frequently directed at the New School: Are we not turning our backs on public education?

This charge seems rhetorical. How "public," to be honest, can we call a system of education dominated by school-board members who do not hear the pleas uttered by a black community? How "public," for a Negro mother, is a white-run school in which a principal will not even allow her to know the reading level of her child for fear of letting her in on the secret that the school, in fact, is teaching nothing? Seen against such history, the community-school venture represents the very fullest blossoming of authentic "public" education. The public bought the building, the public built the playground, the public chose the faculty and the public raised to money. . . .

Some of the basic reservations frequently voiced about the entire community-school venture have to do with the problems of funding, supervision and restrictions.

Clearly, any major expansion of the "community-school" idea is going to require a great deal of federal money. If the experiment is ever to be attempted on a national level, or even on a serious scale in just a dozen separate cities, legislation will have to make it possible for an independent school to get the tax money that the city would ordinarily allocate to the education of the pupils who attend it. Or perhaps in the long run it will be possible for parents who have children in any sort of independent school to receive tax abatement. If something like this happens we will end up with essentially an open market in education, with free and equal competition between what has traditionally been called "public" and what has been called "private" schooling.

Naturally, with funding on such a scale, there will have to be a considerable amount of control and supervision. The Federal Government has numerous restrictions of this sort in effect already for OEO programs and for those generated by the Office of Education. It will be simple enough to set up, in much the same fashion, a number of guidelines dictating the kinds of schools which can or cannot get this kind of per-pupil allocation of tax money. Surely the Government will wish to specify a number of health and safety regulations. Along with these ordinary matters could be included more important regulations concerning racial, ethnic and economic balance. There will be those who might object to such control. White segregationists, or black extremists, interpreting "community" to mean "people exactly like us who live only in our neighborhood," may demand that the Federal Government pay for only the kinds of school these "communities" would like to have. But most concerned people in both the white and black communities can live with sensible regulations. (Whether or not religious qualifications should be a factor in determining which children may attend such schools is another issue again, and one that will call for considerable discussion. Perhaps this question, in the final event, will have to be determined by the courts, rather than by Congress or the people.)

What Do You Think? _____

"Organized education was developed because parents are not qualified to educate." What do you think about the statement after reading "Let The Ghetto Run Its Own Schools"?

3. All Power to the Parents?*

In this article the author recommends that parents be allowed a greater degree of choice in the education of their children. Would you support these ideas? Are they practical?

*Richard Kamman, "The Case for Making Each School in Your District 'Different' and Letting Parents Choose the One That's Best for Their Child." Reprinted, with permission, from *The American School Board Journal,* January 1972. Copyright 1972, the National School Boards Association. All rights reserved.

Imagine a town where every family is assigned arbitrarily to one local doctor by a ruling of the board of health. Imagine that the board of health assigns families only on the basis of the shortest distance from the home to the doctor's office. Imagine, finally, that when a family complains that the assigned doctor is not helping one of its ailing members, the board of health replies: "Sorry, no exceptions to doctor assignments."

If this sounds like a totalitarian nightmare, it is also a description of the way school boards assign children to schools and teachers. As an alternative to the controversial "voucher plans"[1] now under experimentation, why can't school boards create a plan for family choice *within the public schools?* And —before worrying about how to implement such a plan—why *should* families be given a choice? Because the idea makes sense. Simply stated, diversity in educational programs and practices is the raw material for innovation and progress. Moreover, and more to the point, a choice among truly different educational approaches would satisfy the diverse requirements and values of our society in a way not possible right now. Other reasons exist, and not least among them is the residual effect of assuring parents that they have some effective say in their children's education and an alternative if things don't work out in one school—with that kind of reassurance they will be more likely to support budgets and referendums.

The crucial question, it seems to me, is whether a family choice plan can be worked out in practice. To answer it, we can sketch three possible levels of implementation and evaluate the feasibility[2] of each one. The order of the plans discussed here is from the strongest level to the weakest one.

Plan 1—Full implementation. The school board begins by conducting a careful survey of parental goals and educational values. It translates its findings into several distinct educational programs that might be offered at various . . . schools. . . .

Once a child is assigned to a school (and to a program and particular teachers), he is expected to stay there for a year except, perhaps, in specially approved cases of transfer.

The board reinforces the individuality of these schools, each with its distinct approach, by giving each school its own operating budget. This money is under the control of the teaching staff. . . . The board continues to pay all salaries and to make all major purchases.

That, in brief, is the idea—and any experienced board member or administrator will spot a whole zoo of beastly problems in it.

First, will teachers agree to participate in a program like this?

That depends on the trust between the teachers and the board, on whether the teachers have been involved in developing the plan, and on whether they have some say about their own assignments. . . .

---

[1]Voucher plans frequently advocated would provide for parents to receive a certain sum each year for the education of their children. They could then spend this money, in the form of an educational "voucher," in the school of their choice.

[2]Likelihood of success.

Will teachers be equipped to meet the requirements of new educational approaches?

Perhaps not in the most innovative cases, but through special courses, workshops, and inservice training (which they help to develop), they can grow into the job.

Won't parental choices in subsequent years reflect on the performance of individual teachers, and won't this turn into popularity contests?

If the votes of parents can be traced accurately to judgments about a given teacher, they *should* be considered in that teacher's evaluation, along with other factors. . . .

Wouldn't the cost of transporting school children all over the town be prohibitively high?

This will depend heavily on geographic and demographic circumstances. But consider, first, that the most popular kinds of programs could be duplicated in different neighborhoods; second, that each program would be located in the building most central to the majority of its clients; third, that parents generally will take distance into account in deciding among programs, and, fourth, bus transportation in some states is heavily subsidized by the state government. . . .

Plan 2—Autonomous schools. The "full implementation" plan just discussed is structured around clusters of family interests. It can produce more than one program or "mini-school" within a building. Plan 1, therefore, requires *maximum adaptation and accountability* by the teachers. Plan 2—the "autonomous schools" plan—preserves the present building-principal form of administration. The principals and their staffs develop an educational program they consider to be exciting and contemporary. As in Plan 1 (full implementation), they have control over their local operating budgets. Teachers finding their own values out-voted are allowed to request transfers to other schools.

In this system parents are given the option to elect a more distant school, although fewer probably would take this option than under Plan 1. . . .

In this more educator-oriented approach to alternatives, too many parents may want to get their children into one school and too few into another. The solution is a lottery selection among those applying for the too-popular program. Those who are forced to accept a second choice one year are given priority over new candidates for the preferred school the next year.

Plan 3—Choice within the neighborhood school. Plan 2 still has the problem of higher transportation costs. When this problem is serious enough to become a roadblock, the board should consider Plan 3 family choices among mini-schools *within* the nearest neighborhood school building.

These mini-schools consist of teacher teams that agree to define themselves as a unit with particular educational approaches. These are based on teacher interests, parent values, or a joint effort. Again, the matching between programs and family choices might require a lottery system of selection among competing candidates.

The chief problem of the within-school choice plan is that it is limited to **63** small numbers of teachers and students and thus has less flexibility. But there is nothing to prevent a school of 800 students from dividing into three sections of 400, 300, and 100 students each or into any other combination producing two or three mini-schools. The crucial element remains. Each year parents have an opportunity to state their preferences and to have them honored.

No matter what form of family choice plan is adopted, the school board remains responsible for preventing discrimination on the basis of race, ethnic background, social class, or sex. Consequently, it may have to place upper and lower limits on the representation of minority groups in any particular educational program. There are other kinds of "minority groups" among children: children who are classed as slow learners, retarded, neurologically impaired, emotionally disturbed, scientifically gifted. Pressure is increasing on local school systems to make adequate provision for these children and to put them in the hands of educational specialists. The counter-argument is that school should neither be so age-graded nor so competitive that these children must be isolated from their peers.

* * * * *

One more thing. So far the discussion has accepted the conventional wisdom that parents should make decisions for their children. As children grow they should have more and more to say about which school or program is best for them. In many families this will happen anyhow, but the board should do what it can to encourage it in all families.

Now, if you say that the family choice plan is impossible, well, then, of course, it is.

What Do You Think?

1. "The crucial question, it seems to me, is whether a family choice plan can be worked out in practice." What is your opinion?
2. Why limit freedom of choice to public schools alone? Why not let private schools —religious or secular—compete for parents' vouchers?
3. Should students have any say in selecting what school they go to? How serious a say?

4. What about Teachers?*

Next, an argument against providing students with too much freedom.

*B. F. Skinner, "The Free and Happy Student," *Phi Delta Kappan,* September 1973, pp. 13–16. Reprinted by permission in an abridged form from *New York University Education Quarterly,* IV, 2 (Winter 1973):2–6.

His name is Emile. He was born in the middle of the eighteenth century in the first flush of the modern concern for personal freedom. His father was Jean-Jacques Rousseau, but he has had many foster parents, among them Pestalozzi, Froebel, and Montessori, down to A. S. Neill and Ivan Illich.[1] He is an ideal student. Full of good will toward his teachers and peers, he needs no discipline. He studies because he is naturally curious. He learns things because they interest him.

Unfortunately, he is imaginary. . . . Occasionally a real example seems to turn up. There are teachers who would be successful in dealing with people anywhere—as statesmen, therapists, businessmen, or friends—and there are students who scarcely need to be taught, and together they sometimes seem to bring Emile to life. And unfortunately they do so just often enough to sustain the old dream. But Emile is a will-o'-the-wisp, who has led many teachers into a conception of their role which could prove disastrous.

The student who has been taught *as if he were Emile* is, however, almost too painfully real. It has taken a long time for him to make his appearance. Children were first made free and happy in kindergarten, where there seemed to be no danger in freedom, and for a long time they were found nowhere else, because the rigid discipline of the grade schools blocked progress. But eventually they broke through—moving from kindergarten into grade school, taking over grade after grade, moving into secondary school and on into college and, very recently, into graduate school. Step by step they have insisted upon their rights, justifying their demands with the slogans that philosophers of education have supplied. If sitting in rows restricts personal freedom, unscrew the seats. If order can be maintained only through coercion, let chaos reign. If one cannot be really free while worrying about examinations and grades, down with examinations and grades! The whole Establishment is now awash with free and happy students.

If they are what Rousseau's Emile would really have been like, we must confess to some disappointment. The Emile we know doesn't work very hard. "Curiosity" is evidently a moderate sort of thing. Hard work is frowned upon because it implies a "work ethic," which has something to do with discipline.

The Emile we know doesn't learn very much. His "interests" are evidently of limited scope. Subjects that do not appeal to him he calls irrelevant. "We should not be surprised at this, since Rousseau's Emile, like the boys in Summerhill,[2] never got past the stage of knowledgeable craftsman." He may defend himself by questioning the value of knowledge. Knowledge is always in flux, so why bother to acquire any particular stage of it? It will be enough to remain curious and interested. In any case the life of feeling and emotion is to be preferred to the life of intellect; let us be governed by the heart rather than the head.

The Emile we know doesn't think very clearly. He has had little or no chance to learn to think logically or scientifically and is easily taken in by

[1]Educational philosophers.
[2]An experimental school founded by A. S. Neill.

the mystical and the superstitious. Reason is irrelevant to feeling and emotion.

And, alas, the Emile we know doesn't seem particularly happy. He doesn't like his education any more than his predecessors liked theirs. Indeed, he seems to like it less. He is much more inclined to play truant (big cities have given up enforcing truancy laws), and he drops out as soon as he legally can, or a little sooner. If he goes to college, he probably takes a year off at some time in his four-year program. And after that his dissatisfaction takes the form of anti-intellectuality and a refusal to support education.

Are there offsetting advantages? Is the free and happy student less aggressive, kinder, more loving? Certainly not toward the schools and teachers that have set him free, as increasing vandalism and personal attacks on teachers seem to show. Nor is he particularly well disposed toward his peers. He seems perfectly at home in a world of unprecedented domestic violence.

Is he perhaps more creative? Traditional practices were said to suppress individuality; what kind of individuality has now emerged? Free and happy students are certainly different from the students of a generation ago, but they are not very different from each other. Their own culture is a severely regimented one, and their creative works—in art, music, and literature—are confined to primitive and elemental materials. They have very little to be creative with, for they have never taken the trouble to explore the fields in which they are now to be front-runners.

Is the free and happy student at least more effective as a citizen? Is he a better person? The evidence is not very reassuring. Having dropped out of school, he is likely to drop out of life too. It would be unfair to let the hippie culture represent young people today, but it does serve to clarify an extreme. The members of that culture do not accept responsibility for their own lives.
. . .

These are no doubt overstatements. Things are not that bad, nor is education to be blamed for all the trouble. Nevertheless, there is a trend in a well-defined direction, and it is particularly clear in education. Our failure to create a truly free and happy student is symptomatic of a more general problem.

What we may call the struggle for freedom in the Western world can be analyzed as a struggle to escape from or avoid punitive[3] or coercive treatment. It is characteristic of the human species to act in such a way as to reduce or terminate irritating, painful, or dangerous stimuli, and the struggle for freedom has been directed toward those who would control others with stimuli of that sort. Education has had a long and shameful part in the history of that struggle. The Egyptians, Greeks, and Romans all whipped their students. Medieval sculpture showed the carpenter with his hammer and the schoolmaster with the tool of his trade too, and it was the cane or rod. We are not yet in the clear. Corporal punishment is still used in many schools, and there are calls for its return where it has been abandoned.

66   [3]Punishing.

A system in which students study primarily to avoid the consequences of not studying is neither humane nor very productive. Its by-products include truancy, vandalism, and apathy. Any effort to eliminate punishment in education is certainly commendable. . . . They should study because they want to, because they like to, because they are interested in what they are doing. The mistake—a classical mistake in the literature of freedom—is to suppose that they will do so as soon as we stop punishing them. Students are not literally free when they have been freed from their teachers. They then simply come under the control of other conditions, and we must look at those conditions and their effects if we are to improve teaching.

Those who have attacked the "servility" of students, as Montessori called it, have often put their faith in the possibility that young people will learn what they need to know from the "world of things," which includes the world of people who are not teachers. . . . [Such a proposition ignores two vital points.]

1. No one learns very much from the real world without help. . . . Much more can be learned without formal instruction in a social world, but not without a good deal of teaching, even so. Formal education has made a tremendous difference in the extent of the skills and knowledge which can be acquired by a person in a single lifetime.

2. A much more important principle is that the real world teaches only what is relevant to the present; it makes no explicit preparation for the future. Those who would minimize teaching have contended that no preparation is needed, that the student will follow a natural line of development and move into the future in a normal course of events. . . .

But it has always been the task of formal education to set up behavior which would prove useful or enjoyable *later* in the student's life. Punitive methods had at least the merit of providing current reasons for learning things that would be rewarding in the future. We object to the punitive reasons, but we should not forget their function in making the future important.

It is not enough to give the student advice—to explain that he will have a future, and that to enjoy himself and be more successful in it, he must acquire certain skills and knowledge now. Mere advice is ineffective because it is not supported by current rewards. The positive consequences that generate a useful behavioral repertoire[4] need not be any more explicitly relevant to the future than were the punitive consequences of the past. The student needs current reasons, positive or negative, but only the educational policy maker who supplies them need take the future into account. It follows that many instructional arrangements seem "contrived," but there is nothing wrong with that. It is the teacher's function to contrive conditions under which students learn. Their relevance to a future usefulness need not be obvious.

It is a difficult assignment. The conditions the teacher arranges must be powerful enough to compete with those under which the student tends to behave in distracting ways. In what has come to be called "contingency

4Special skills.   **67**

in specifying what students are to learn, we do not absolve ourselves from the responsibility of setting educational policy. We should say, we should be management in the classroom," tokens[5] are sometimes used as rewards or reinforcers. They become reinforcing when they are exchanged for reinforcers that are already effective. There is no "natural" relation between what is learned and what is received. The token is simply a reinforcer that can be made clearly contingent upon behavior. To straighten out a wholly disrupted classroom, something as obvious as a token economy may be needed, but less conspicuous contingencies—as in a credit-point system, perhaps, or possibly in the long run merely expressions of approval on the part of teacher or peer —may take over.

The teacher can often make the change from punishment to positive reinforcement in a surprisingly simple way—by responding to the student's success rather than his failures. . . . Programmed materials are helpful in bringing about these changes, because they increase the frequency with which the student enjoys the satisfaction of being right, and they supply a valuable intrinsic[6] reward in providing a clear indication of progress. A good program makes a step in the direction of competence almost as conspicuous as a token.

Programmed instruction is perhaps most successful in attacking punitive methods by allowing the student to move at his own pace. The slow student is released from the punishment which inevitably follows when he is forced to move on to material for which he is not ready, and the fast student escapes the boredom of being forced to go too slow. . . .

There is little doubt that a student can be given nonpunitive reasons for acquiring behavior that will become useful or otherwise reinforcing at some later date. He can be prepared for the future. But what *is* that future? Who is to say what the student should learn? Those who have sponsored the free and happy student have argued that it is the student himself who should say. His current interests should be the source of an effective educational policy. Certainly they will reflect his idiosyncrasies,[7] and that is good, but how much can he know about the world in which he will eventually play a part? The things he is "naturally" curious about are of current and often temporary interest. How many things must he possess besides his "hot rod" to provide the insatiable curiosity relevant to, say, a course in physics?

It must be admitted that the teacher is not always in a better position. Again and again education has gone out of date as teachers have continued to teach subjects which were no longer relevant at any time in the student's life. Teachers often teach simply what they know. (Much of what is taught in private schools is determined by what the available teachers can teach.) Teachers tend to teach what they can teach easily. Their current interests, like those of students, may not be a reliable guide.

Nevertheless, in recognizing the mistakes that have been made in the past

---

[5]Something that is given for success in learning.
[6]Internal.
[7]Personal peculiarities.

willing to say, what we believe students will need to know, taking the individual student into account wherever possible, but otherwise making our best prediction with respect to students in general. . . .

The natural, logical outcome of the struggle for personal freedom in education is that the teacher should improve his control of the student rather than abandon it. The free school is no school at all. Its philosophy signalizes the abdication of the teacher. The teacher who understands his assignment and is familiar with the behavioral processes needed to fulfill it can have students who not only feel free and happy while they are being taught but who will continue to feel free and happy when their formal education comes to an end. They will do so because they will be successful in their work (having acquired useful productive repertoires), because they will get on well with their fellows (having learned to understand themselves and others), because they will enjoy what they do (having acquired the necessary knowledge and skills), and because they will from time to time make an occasional creative contribution toward an even more effective and enjoyable way of life. Possibly the most important consequence is that the teacher will then feel free and happy too.

We must choose today between Cassandran and Utopian[8] prognostications.[9] Are we to work to avoid disaster or to achieve a better world? Again, it is a question of punishment or reward. Must we act because we are frightened, or are there positive reasons for changing our cultural practices? The issue goes far beyond education, but it is one with respect to which education has much to offer. To escape from or avoid disaster, people are likely to turn to the punitive measures of a police state. To work for a better world, they may turn instead to the positive methods of education. When it finds its most effective methods, education will be almost uniquely relevant to the task of setting up and maintaining a better way of life.

What Do You Think? _____

1. Who is the "free and happy" student Skinner describes?
2. Does your educational experience square with Skinner's descriptions?
3. What kind of teachers does Skinner argue are needed to teach successfully?
4. Suppose you wanted to argue *against* Skinner; what would you say?

---

5. Who's in Charge Here?

There is no easy answer to the question, "Who Should Run the Schools?" As you consider the following cartoons, ask yourself what they are saying about power in the school setting.

[8]Overly pessimistic or optimistic.
[9]Predictions.

" '... and we demand a ... more relevant ... education.' Do you spell education with one k or two?"

© Dow Jones, permission
The Wall Street Journal.

"She's got a lot to learn."
Reg Hilder from
Today's Education, March 1972.

"As an administrative assistant, one of your jobs is to see that the school board doesn't come poking its nose in here."
Ford Button in *Phi Delta Kappan,* September 1974.

"It might help if we stopped referring to the faculty as 'us' and the students as 'them.'"

Ford Button in
Phi Delta Kappan, September 1974.

"You'd better go to school tomorrow and see how things are.... he prayed for his teacher tonight!"

Joe E. Buresch from *Today's Education,* April 1971.

What Do You Think? ————————————————

1. What are the limits to student control? In what areas do you think students should enjoy meaningful power in the school?

2. As teachers become better educated and better organized, will they continue to accept the traditional role of executor of policy in schools?

3. What would it take to get a faculty to stop thinking of themselves as "we" and the students as "they"? Would that be a good idea?

4. Whom do you think run the schools? Students? Faculty? Parents? The community as a whole? School boards? Administrators? Some combination of these? Explain your reasoning.

ACTIVITIES FOR INVOLVEMENT

1. People who responded to the Sixth Annual Gallup Poll of Public Attitudes Toward Education (1974) placed "lack of discipline" at the head of the list of major problems confronting the public schools. It has been identified as the number-one problem for five of the last six years. An even higher percentage of high school juniors and seniors named discipline as the leading problem.
   Other problems, listed in order, are
   2. Integration/segregation.
   3. Lack of proper financial support.
   4. Use of drugs.
   5. Difficulty in getting "good" teachers.
   6. Size of school/classes.
   7. Parents' lack of interest.
   8. School board policies.
   9. Poor curriculum.
   10. Lack of proper facilities.
   Conduct a similar poll in your school to determine what, in the view of students and teachers, are the major problems facing public schools.

2. Attend one of the meetings of the Board of Education of your school district. What kinds of issues are dealt with? In what ways? What kinds of issues should be dealt with?

3. On the basis of your study, draw up a plan for the government of your school district that would best reflect the interests of parents, teachers, community groups, and students. What means of control would you devise? What would be your major problems? What methods of ensuring clear and easy communication would you design?

4. Consider the possibility of electing some under-twenty-one-year-old school board members in your district. What kind of candidates would you look for? How might you find them? What would need to be done to ensure a broad-based support for such a candidate?

5. Interview your superintendent of schools to determine his or her view of the problems and opportunities of the superintendent's position. What has

been the record of superintendents in your district? How do you account for their leaving office? For their selection?

6. B. F. Skinner mentions a number of important writers on education, including A. S. Neill, Pestalozzi, Rousseau, and Ivan Illich. He has also made reference to the works of Paul Goodman, John Holt, Jonathan Kozol, and Charles Silberman. Undertake a research project to determine the major views of such writers. What do they have to say? Which ones impress you the most? Why?

7. Interview a number of teachers concerning the question of teacher power. How much power do they want? Now interview a number of parents and other adults in your community. How much power are they willing for teachers to have? If there are differences, how might these be resolved?

8. There is no mention in this chapter of "student control" on the high school level. Listed below are a number of suggestions as to ways in which students might exercise control. Which would you endorse, and why?

    (a) Determining menus for the school cafeteria.
    (b) Teaching younger students.
    (c) Selecting textbooks and other curricular materials.
    (d) Landscaping the school grounds.
    (e) Hiring and firing teachers.
    (f) Hiring and firing administrators.

Rank these in order from most to least important. What would you add to the list?

6
CIVIL LIBERTIES AND THE SCHOOLS

To what extent do the schools attempt to regulate student and teacher dress, speech, and behavior? To what extent are such attempts legal? Few would argue that the schools do *not* need some power in this regard. The question, however, is how much. This chapter presents several views on this question, along with examples of actions by schools and school boards in attempting to regulate behavior, and the reaction of students and teachers to these attempts.

1. A Student Poses Some Hard Questions*

First, one student expresses his outrage at what he considers "phoniness" on the part of the school.

"At the beginning of the second period, students in John Marshall Senior High School will stand to recite the Pledge of Allegiance, while facing the national emblem. Upon receipt, in writing, of a parent's request, a student may be excused from recitation of the pledge, but not from the obligation to stand silently during the ceremony." *Administrative Code, Section 104.2, adopted by the Board of Education January 16, 1952.*

The following Letter to the Editor was written by a student who would not comply with a long-standing school regulation. In addition, he was the only student in the history of John Marshall Senior High School to object to the regulation.

The letter reflects a particular point of view. Is Charles Rasmussen correct in his position? What are the major questions raised by such a controversy?

To the Editor,
John Marshall *Vindicator*

Dear Sir:
For the past two weeks I have been suspended from school for the magnificently simple-minded reason that I refused for three days running

*Gordon M. Seely.

to stand up during the flag salute in Mr. Fred Cherry's second period. Despite the fact the class is supposed to be studying American institutions, I have found a rather colossal failure on anybody's part to even try to understand my reasons. My glorious counselor, Mrs. Fritzie Evans, even asked me at one point in the proceedings if I didn't think I needed "help." I take this opportunity to announce that I am not crazy. Fritzie, take a bow.

At the present moment, I am so damn upset with my country that I would be a fake and a supreme fraud to stand up and salute its symbol. Maybe some day, but not now. . . .

I can't find anything in the Declaration of Independence or in the Constitution that says I've got to give a salute to the flag with my mouth or by assuming the vertical position. In the "land of the free" a guy should be able to sit, to lie, to stand, or to take five when it comes to public ceremonies.

Mr. Cherry admits he can't find anything in the Constitution about flag salutes. The best he could do was to quote Justice Felix Frankfurter, who wrote in *Minersville v. Gobitis* 310 U.S. 585:

> That which to the majority may seem essential for the welfare of the state may offend the consciences of a minority. But, so long as no inroads are made upon the actual exercise of religion by the minority, to deny the political power of the majority to enact laws concerned with civil matters, simply because they may offend the consciences of a minority, really means that the consciences of a minority are more sacred than the consciences of a majority.

Well, that was in 1939, and I wasn't even born. Anyway, Justice Robert Jackson wrote in 1942 in *West Virginia v. Barnette* 319 U.S. 624:

> If there is any fixed star in our constitutional constellation, it is that no official, high or petty, can prescribe what shall be orthodox in politics, nationalism, religion, or other matters of opinion or force citizens to confess by word or act their faith therein.

I wasn't born then either, but I like the ideas better. By the way, I highly recommend the public library for research when you are barred from the campus.

To all my friends and admirers, including the three jocks who roughed me up last week, I hereby announce I'll probably be back next week, saluting on my aching feet, because at this point I want to get out of dear old John Marshall so bad I'll step on my principles to do it. But I want everybody to know how phony the whole thing is, and how little a guy's opinion really counts around here.

Charles S. Rasmussen

P.S. Mr. Cherry did give me an A in research techniques.

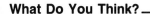
Was Charles justified in what he did? Why or why not? On what grounds?

2. "You Bought a House Next to Mellon High?—You've Flipped!"*

The civil rights of many groups are involved in a school—students, teachers, and citizens. The following exchange of correspondence raises many questions regarding student freedoms and citizens' rights to enjoy their homes if they happen to live next to a school.

Dear Mr. Fletcher,
Principal, Andrew J. Mellon Junior High School

Before taking the matter to the police, I am writing you for your help. Perhaps you and your student government can find a solution to my problem.

I live at the corner of Jenkins and Criterion, directly across from your school. At lunch time my front lawn becomes a meeting place for students eating lunch, visiting, and enjoying a cigarette. I have counted as many as twenty students at one time on my lawn.

At one o'clock everyday I begin my clean-up chores. It takes me about a half hour to pick up the discarded papers, cans, and cigarette butts. I wouldn't even estimate the amount of time I spend trying to keep my lawn in decent condition.

Too often, I feel, older people appear to youngsters as crabs. I wonder, however, if I am asking too much for students to respect my property by eating lunch in public places, and not littering. I hear a great deal about youngsters' interest in ecology—could it maybe begin at the corner of Jenkins and Criterion?

Sincerely,
Thelma Langlois

Dear Mrs. Langlois
Thank you for your recent letter. I am sorry to learn of your problem with Mellon students and your front lawn.

We wish that it were possible for us to keep Mellon students on the campus during the noon hour. As you may know, our effort to do just that was nullified by an opinion of the District Attorney to the effect that we could not so restrict the freedom of our students. The opinion was sought, in fact,

*Gordon M. Seely.

by a group of local merchants who cater to the lunch-time needs of the youngsters.

Smoking is forbidden by state law on the campus. Possession of tobacco by minors is also forbidden. I do not need to tell you that we have our hands full controlling the problem on campus. I could not hope to control things even a short distance away from the school.

I have discussed your letter with our student body officers, and they intend to take up the entire subject of the relations of Mellon students to our neighbors. Many youngsters—in fact, most—wish to be good neighbors.

I cannot ask you not to take your problem to the police, because it is obvious laws are being broken. I will ask you to give us and our student officers a little time to work on a plan of education and persuasion. I know you have already been patient.

Yours very truly,
Twohig A. McQueen, Principal

What Do You Think? _____

1. What are the "rights and wrongs" in the situation described in these two letters?

2. What are the limits of school authority in regulating student's off-campus behavior? Should students be restricted to a campus during the school day?

3. The cartoon below appeared in *The Wall Street Journal.* How serious is the problem of vandalism in neighborhoods near schools? How does such a situation, assuming it exists, affect support for schools? Is there anything youngsters in school can do to correct the situation?

"I know you'll like the location—just a stone's throw away from schools."

3. Girls and Civil Rights*

In most cases involving civil rights in the schools, violations are out in the open and easy to see. In this article, a sensitive teacher considers the rights of her female students to fair and equal treatment. Does the problem go beyond the situation she describes with the potting wheel?

No girl would get away with the kind of behavior Bill shows in my class. He is aggressive, even rude at times, and sprawls all over the chair as if he owned the world (maybe he does). But he has good ideas. I picture him as he may be twenty or thirty years from now—respected, listened to, a brilliant man who has made his mark in some intellectual field or another. Eccentric, yes —egotistical, yes, but forgiven this because of his indubitable achievement. I find myself liking him in spite of myself.

I teach ceramics and jewelry in high school and junior high. Bill is taking ceramics. Yesterday in class he grabbed a tool from a girl at another table. I took it from him and gave it back to the girl. "Ask first," I said. "Kin I have it," said Bill rudely and grabbed the tool again as the girl started to say she needed it. I gave the tool once more to the girl—and found another one for Bill.

The next time around he was more polite. Not an incorrigible.[1] Good thing he likes my class—what a troublemaker he'd be if he didn't! Two years ago I would not have given the matter another thought—boys will be boys after all. Now I wonder.

Bill is a freshman. Before he finishes high school some of the rougher edges will have worn off, but the essential man is there already. Bill is my best ceramics student this year. He is the one with the ideas, the one who tests the limits of my own knowledge, the one who tries the large abstract sculptures and the vase that just barely fits in the kiln. Later in the year the class will no doubt follow suit, but he is the one who starts things.

Could a girl be like that? I can't imagine one. There are girls and women who are aggressive of course, but it seems to me always in a more covert[2] way, with an unspoken apology as if to say, "Excuse me for being aggressive but . . ." (Is it this hidden quality that makes aggressive women so often unpleasant? or is it our expectations of women that make them so?) or with flirtatiousness to mask the aggressiveness. Not with that easy self-assurance. Not with that open and unrepentant defiance.

And if there were a girl like that? Well, to begin with, no one would like her—I don't suppose I would like her myself. By the time she reached high

*Nella Fermi Weiner, "Sugar and Spice," *School Review,* November 1972, University of Chicago Press.
[1]A person who cannot be reformed.
[2]Hidden.

school it would no doubt be all out of her, or have turned to resentment. Now that I think of it, some little girls are like that. Behavior like this from a girl is seriously frowned upon. From a boy it is laughingly frowned upon.

Still, is Bill a model worth emulating?[3] Perhaps not, but the inequity is there. And if you curb bad behavior too much, will creativity go too? Why did the girl give up the tool so easily? And if you think sugar and spice leave something to be desired, do you necessarily endorse snips and snails?

My eighth-grade class is working on a ceramic tile mural. The project involves five panels, each one made by a group of four or five. The students chose their own groupings. Three of the groups are all girls, one is all boys, and one is mixed. There is not enough room for everyone at the tables so that two of the groups work on the floor—both are girls' groups. No one minds working on the floor, but how did it happen? Not everyone in a group can work from the same side of a panel, so some are working upside down. The boys' panel is so abstract it's hard to tell who's upside down. I think perhaps they're all working right side up.

Four of the groups work in harmony. The mixed group squabbles—or, to be more exact, two of the three boys are squabbling with each other. The two girls in this group are very adept at patching up the differences but so unsure of themselves that they are unaware of their effectiveness and keep appealing to me for help in dealing with the situation. I tell them they can cope and they do.

Girls are more mature. Everybody knows that. More socially adept?—well certainly more socially adept. But more mature? Is it mature to need so much reassurance? Bill's work shows a great deal of maturity even if his social adaptation does not. So often it is a boy who is doing the really outstanding work in my classes even though I teach more girls than boys. There is a bias here. It would be a boy with a very strong interest in the subject that would take jewelry or ceramics from a woman rather than shop or photography from a man. But if I went into the shop would I find that those few girls taking shop are as outstanding?

When the girls do good work, often they seem to want to cover up the fact with false modesty or not even to recognize that it is good work. The boys more often seem to expect their work to be appreciated and since to an extent we get the response we ask for, I might tend to overestimate the boys' work and underestimate the girls'. Surely this would inhibit the girls, the more so if they had become used to being underestimated. A cyclic[4] reaction.

Ann is sitting in my room after school sawing a silver pin of an intricate pattern. Her boyfriend (who has never taken jewelry) is sitting next to her kibitzing. He tells her she's not sawing straight and why can't she do it right. His tone is bantering and Ann takes it with good humor. But later she gives up making the pin because she feels she has done too poor a job of sawing. It's rare that a jewelry project is given up in the middle. The silver is expensive and paid for by the student. Often it's possible to correct mistakes or change

[3]Imitating.
80 [4]Circular.

the original plan to salvage the piece. Ann's sawing is by no means as bad as she thinks, and I try to encourage her to continue her project, but to no avail.

Of a sudden I am back in seventh grade myself—a new kid in the school —as it happens the same school where I now teach. One of the boys teased me—hostilely as it seemed to me and I reacted with hostility. Later that year a teacher (male, but perhaps that's not important) explained to the class that teasing was the boys' way of making their first advances (we didn't talk about sex in those days) toward the girls and that their apparent hostility was a mask for their interest and uncertainty. I understood my mistake, but it was too late. I was teased no more. Later still the same boy was chasing the most popular girl in the class, threatening to put an insect down her back. She was running, screaming, but obviously enjoying it. I thought then, as I do now, that she had made a fool of herself. But from that day to this I have been afraid of insects.

Things have not changed much. The boys wear long hair. the girls wear jeans and longer hair and sometimes skirts down to the floor. Underneath, the old differences persist.

There was an undertone of sexuality in Bill's taking of the tool, and while the girl did not want to give it up she did not know how to defend it.

I wish I had thought to hand Ann's boyfriend a saw and ask him if he could do better. Dollars to doughnuts he would have done worse—Ann is good at jewelry.

The new potter's wheel came unassembled so that when I was assigning jobs one day (wash tables, straighten shelves) I cast my eye about the room for boys to whom I could assign the job of putting it together. And then, having realized what I was doing, I gave the job to three girls. They informed me flatly that they did not know how. I handed them the instructions and said I would help them if they needed it. When they were done (no help) they were delighted. "It shows," said one, "what girls can do if they put their minds to it."

That was an easy one and yet I almost flubbed it. What about the hard ones?

What Do You Think? _____

1. Did this teacher have anything to worry about in her handling of her students?
2. Does the sex of students prejudice teachers in their expectation of student ability? In every field?

4. Civil Rights and Fairness—A Delicate Balance

The following articles deal with the problem of fairness in admission to schools and in testing for admission or advancement. What is at stake in these situations?

A. Instead of Quotas*

Last Sunday in this space I expressed some concern about where the quota system is taking us.

I said it is basically an attempt at compensatory discrimination; that it is more likely to institutionalize discrimination than to end it; that it encourages minority groups to resist assimilation and retain their separate identity in order to keep their quotas.

I said I wished I could offer an effective alternative to the quota system, but I didn't have one.

Among those who read those remarks was Joel Brooks, director of the American Jewish Congress, which has its own alternative to the quota system.

"The American Jewish community is faced with a unique dilemma regarding quotas," Brooks said. "During the 1930s quotas were used extensively by universities and colleges to 'keep people out'. . . . Today, quotas are being used extensively, and have the support of our government, to 'bring people in.'

"Unfortunately what has happened all too frequently is when you set up a quota to bring people in, by the very reason of it being a quota it will keep others out."

Their own long struggle for equal treatment conditioned Jews to sympathize with the struggle by the black and brown minorities.

But the two struggles were basically different, as Mr. Brooks' remarks suggest, and the great test for Jewish sentiment came with the Marco DeFunis case.

DeFunis was a bright boy. He worked 40 hours a week while going to college and still made Phi Beta Kappa. But when he sought to enroll in law school he was turned down, while 36 minority students with lower scores were accepted.

"If DeFunis had been black he would have been admitted," his lawyer told the Supreme Court. "He was kept out because he was white."

DeFunis also was Jewish, and to many Jews his rejection brought back bitter memories.

A staple of American Jewish folklore is the brilliant boy who never became a doctor because many medical schools used to accept only two or three Jews in each entering class.

The American Jewish Congress had fought to end that crippling quota system. Now a supposedly benign quota system was producing the same result.

While the DeFunis case was moving through the Courts (the Supreme Court eventually sidestepped it) the American Jewish Congress passed an historic resolution. It affirmed its support of equality for racial minorities, but it rejected the quota system.

"We believe such an approach is socially undesirable and does irreparable damage to the concept of justice," it said.

What alternative did it offer? Essentially it called for expanding opportunities for everyone, rather than rationing opportunity by quotas.

It called for training programs, opening up unions, minority job recruit-

*Guy Wright, "Instead of Quotas," *San Francisco Examiner,* July 14, 1974.

ment, vigorous enforcement of anti-discrimination laws, insistence that hiring tests be job-related and free of cultural bias.

But it made ability the sine qua non[1]:

"Only applicants who meet the minimum and reasonable qualifications applicable to all . . . will be regarded as eligible.

"Goals (for minority hiring) may be established only on the basis of a bona fide[2] finding as to available qualified talent in the disadvantaged group . . . and not on the basis of the proportion of disadvantaged group members to the population as a whole."

Whether that resolution is an acceptable alternative to the quota system I don't know. But I believe the leaders of the struggle for racial equality would be wise to admit that the quota system isn't the answer and look for something else.

B. Testing Minorities*

You know that poor blacks and other disadvantaged minorities don't do as well on standardized tests as middle-class whites.

You also know that one of the reasons frequently given for this shortcoming is "cultural bias"—that is, the tests either don't ask questions based on the knowledge that the minorities have accumulated, or they ask them in such a way that the minorities show less knowledge than they have.

But if the standardized tests are biased against certain minorities on these counts, it certainly ought to be possible to construct tests that are biased *toward* these same minorities: tests that are based on the peculiar life-styles of the big-city ghetto, for instance, and administered in ways that will show ghetto test-takers to advantage.

Dr. Robert L. Williams, professor of psychology and head of the black studies program at Washington University, St. Louis, has a modest example: the BITCH test, or Black Intelligence Test of Cultural Homogeneity.

Multiple Choice

His test, about which he is totally serious, consists of 100 multiple-choice questions to be answered as black people would answer them. For example:

1. *Nose opened* means (A) flirting, (B) teed off, (C) deeply in love, (D) very angry.

2. *Blood* means (A) a vampire, (B) a dependent individual, (C) an injured person, (D) a brother of color.

3. *Mother's Day* means (A) black independence day, (B) a day when mothers are honored, (C) a day the welfare checks come in, (D) every first Sunday in church.

[1]Absolutely necessary requirement.
[2]Honest.
*William Raspberry, "Testing Minorities," *Newsweek*, September 23, 1974, p. 19. Copyright Newsweek, Inc. 1974. Reprinted by permission.

4. The following are popular brand names. Which one does not belong? (A) Murray's, (B) Dixie Peach, (C) Royal Crown, (D) Preparation H.

Williams says his research has shown that nearly all blacks who take his BITCH test do better than nearly all whites who take it. He sees that outcome as proof that cultural bias is a manipulable thing that can be made to favor any group the test-makers want it to.

But wait. The tests that are the despair of disadvantaged blacks—the tests that keep them out of the good tracks in school, the good colleges and the good jobs—are those that purport to measure skills, aptitudes, achievement and reasoning ability. Williams's test measures knowledge of a specialized vocabulary.

Except for the fourth question, which calls for recognition of various hair pomades (Preparation H is a treatment for hemorrhoids), all the examples given—and 96 out of the 100 questions on the test—depend on knowledge of ghetto slang. It's like asking whether children, white or black, are familiar with such words as house, car, love or gun and supposing that the answers tell us much about the children's intelligence.

The Problem

I suppose Williams wanted a test that would measure knowledge primarily familiar to black people and on which black people, therefore, would score better than whites. If all you want is for Johnny to outscore the rest of his class, just ask the middle name of Johnny's mother. He'll likely do better than anyone else in the room on that one.

But the problem is not simply to have black people and other minorities pass *some* test. The problem is to pass those tests that tell something about their qualifications to do those things that they would like to do.

A good many of the tests designed to do that are of questionable validity. The person who scores highest on a written test for bricklayers, for instance, might not be the best bricklayer, actual or potential, in the group.

Most job tests should be reconstructed to make them more clearly related to the tasks to be performed. The Federal service entrance examination, for instance, is used to screen applicants for more than 100 different jobs. But since the questions have little to do with the specific skills required for those jobs, it's a safe bet that they screen out a lot of people who could perform well on the job. It's a safe bet, too, that they screen out a disproportionate percentage of potentially competent blacks. There *is* cultural bias you know.

The need is to eliminate those aspects of cultural bias that have nothing to do with what the test is about. If you're hiring cabinetmakers or plumbers, there's not much point in asking questions that measure knowledge of history or English (beyond a basic working familiarity).

But to say that questions on history, English grammar and proverbs are culturally biased is not to say that they should be eliminated from all tests. John David Garcia, director of the Science Education Extension, explains:

"Achievement tests are *supposed* to be culturally biased. Their purpose is to measure how well persons have assimilated particular cultural information and learned to predict and control with this information. For the vast majority of Americans it is essential to be able to predict and control the cultural environment of the white middle class, if they are to have any type of success at all in our society. To dismiss mathematics and reading achievement scores as irrelevant to black children is to do these children a disservice. It is like responding to a fire by putting out the alarm instead of the fire."

The Solution

That is the point that so many critics of standardized tests keep missing. They are dead right in charging that many of the tests are inadequate measures of what they purport to measure, and that some of them—notably the IQ type—may be positively harmful, at least in some of their usages.

But since there are going to be tests for so long as there are more applicants than places, the solution is not to throw out the tests but to insist on making the tests do what they allege to do, and to give minorities the wherewithal to pass them—by teaching them how to pass tests, if necessary.

What Do You Think? _____

1. Should race or ethnic background have anything to do with admission to school? Why or why not? Would the type of school make any difference?

2. Do problems arise when some kind of "compensatory discrimination" is used? If so, what are they?

3. What is the main point of Raspberry's argument? Would you agree? Why or why not?

4. Is a quota system ever justifiable? If so, under what conditions?

---

5. A Student Bill of Rights*

Since young people have won the right to vote, school administrators have become more conscious of students' rights to due process and to fairness in disciplinary matters. The following is an example of an attempt by a school system to clarify student rights and responsibilities. As you read through the article, think about its strengths and weaknesses. What suggestions could you make to improve the policies?

*"Students Rights and Responsibilities," edited version, of *Students Rights and Responsibilities Manual,* San Francisco Unified School District, June 15, 1972.

Students Responsibilities

It is impossible to list all student responsibilities, but it must be emphasized that lack of responsibility means a weakening of rights.
Students have the responsibility to:

1. *Respect* the *rights* of all persons involved in the educational process.
2. Exercise the highest degree of *self-discipline* in observing and adhering to legitimate rules and regulations.
3. Recognize that *responsibility* is *inherent in* the exercise of every *right.*
4. Refrain from actions that will *interfere* with the operation of the regular *school program* or with classroom activities.
5. Refrain from any distribution or display of materials which are *obscene* according to the current legal definitions, which are *libelous* or which *advocate* the commission of *unlawful acts.*

Students Rights

Correspondingly, it is impossible to list all of the rights of students. Therefore, the following list of rights shall not be construed to deny or limit others retained by students on their own campus in their capacity as members of the student body or as citizens.
Students have the right to:

1. A *meaningful education. . . .*
2. The maintenance of *high educational standards. . . .*
3. A *meaningful curriculum* and the right to voice their opinions in the development of such curriculum.
4. *Physical safety* and protection of personal *property.*
5. *Safe buildings* and *sanitary facilities.*
6. *Consultation* with . . . anyone . . . connected with the school.
7. *Free election* of their peers in the student government and the right to seek and hold office.
8. Democratic *representation in administrative committees* affecting students and *student rights.*
9. *Participation* in the development of *rules and regulations* to which they are subject. . . .
10. See their own *personal files,* cumulative folders, transcripts, deans' files, etc. . . .
11. Be involved in *school activities* if they so desire without being subject to discrimination on any basis, provided they meet with the reasonable qualifications of sponsoring organizations.
12. Present *petitions,* complaints or grievances to school authorities. . . .
13. Not be penalized in any way by the school administration for the beliefs they hold provided they do not violate the rights of others.

14. *Respect* from teachers and administrators, which would exclude their being subjected to cruel and unusual punishments, especially those which are demeaning or derogatory or which diminish their self-esteem or exclude them from their peers.
15. Not be searched arbitrarily or to have their lockers, automobiles, or personal belongings subject to *arbitrary searches and seizures.* No student's name, address, or telephone number shall be given without consent of the student. . . .
16. Exercise their constitutionally protected rights of *free speech and assembly* on their own campus. . . . However, students must *refrain* from any distribution or display of materials which are *obscene* according to the current legal definitions, which are *libelous,* or which *advocate* the commission of *unlawful acts.*

California State Education Code Sec. 10611 states the rights of students to:

(a) Wear political buttons, armbands, or any other *badges* of symbolic expression.
(b) Use *bulletin boards* without prior censorship requirements or approval by the administration or the Board of Education.
(c) *Distribute* political leaflets, newspapers, or other *printed matter* both inside and outside of school property without prior authorization of, restriction by, school administration or the Board of Education. . . .
(d) Form *political* and *social organizations.*
(e) Determine their own *appearance* including the style of their hair and clothing.
(f) Reasonable use of *public address systems* in school without prior censorship. . . .

Corporal Punishment

1. No student shall be subject to the infliction of corporal punishment.
2. Anyone on school grounds has the right to use physical means to defend himself or restrain another from damaging real or personal property.

Due Process Appeals Procedure

1. *School Site Student Appeals Board*
Every secondary school shall adopt a workable, effective appeals procedure, involving fairness in the composition and selection of the representation on the Appeals Board. If a student in the *secondary school* feels his rights have been violated by any member of the personnel in his school he may request a hearing before the School Site Appeals Board at his school.

2. *City Wide Student Appeals Board*
The City Wide Student Appeals Board shall have the power and responsibility to:
   (a) Hear appeals by students regarding adverse decisions by the School Site Student Appeals Board.
   (b) Hear appeals on suspensions and minor infractions. *Procedures* and *names* of Appeal Board members should be *posted* where they are *easily available* to students.

What Do You Think?

1. Is the policy statement you just read fair?
2. What would you add to the statement to make it more useful in your school? Delete? Modify?
3. Does the statement appear to protect the rights of teachers and administrators?

---

6. Should the Public Schools Be Godless?

The relation of public schools to religious beliefs has long been a subject of controversy in the United States. Our Constitution protects religious freedom, but our culture strongly supports religious belief. The following two articles exemplify aspects of the problem today.

A. *Discord over Public School Song**

Santa Rosa

"God has to be left in there," Dawn Scherba told the media throng attending her "peaceful assembly" of protest in the Hall of Justice patio here yesterday.

"That little three-letter word that's caused so much trouble—that's the whole point," declared the slight but spunky strawberry blonde, mother of three, Seventh Day Adventist, and defender of the lost cause of keeping praise of God in California's kindergarten curricula.

She had petitions signed by 1400 people endorsing her position, though few had come out in the heat of the day to face the media with her.

At issue was Sonoma County Superior Court Judge Joseph P. Murphy Jr.'s June 11 ruling against public school use of a "Thanksgiving" song that thanked God for various favors.

His precedents were the 1962 and 1963 Supreme Court rulings against

---

*Kevin Wallace, "Discord Over Public School Song," San Francisco *Chronicle,* June 27, 1974. © Chronicle Publishing Co., 1974.

public school prayers as breaches of the Constitution's separation of church and state.

Murphy had said his ruling "will likely irritate people who are rightfully concerned about the decline in today's society."

But, he said, "Singing the song in public school is clearly unconstitutional."

Mrs. Scherba, whose children go to school in nearby Cotati, told the peaceful assembly of reporters and TV crews why she wasn't going to hold still for any mere ruling of unconstitutionality.

"I'm going to take these petitions to the State Department of Education in Sacramento next Monday and ask them to appeal on grounds that this is not a prayer—it's a song.

"And I most certainly wouldn't agree to compromise by removing the word 'God' from the text.

"Keeping God in there is my whole purpose.

"If my children can't share their church experiences in school, and sing a song about God, then what's left but communism, and no more freedom of speech or religion or expression at all?"

She tried to round up her three children to sing the contested song for the TV camera, and two of them turned up—Heidi Michelle, 10, and Richie, 6, accompanied by a friend named Bill Huffman.

Mrs. Scherba's third child, Michael, 9, had made himself scarce.

Heidi Michelle opened the song book—its name is "Making Music Your Own," and it bears the imprint of the California State Department of Education, 1967—and turned to the page labeled "Thanksgiving."

The boy didn't even move his lips, but Heidi Michelle sang brave and true:

"Thank you for the world so sweet/Thank you for the food we eat/Thank you for the birds that sing/Thank you for everything."

The TV cameras ground to a halt.

"Where was God?" asked an irascible crew member.

"I forgot," Heidi Michelle said.

"O.K., we'll do it over," the crew's spokesman said.

They did it over. This time, Heidi Michelle gave the full reading of the last and much litigated line:

"Thank you God for everything."

Lurking in the background was a tall young Santa Rosa lawyer named Martin Spiegel. He had argued for the complaint that had been brought March 11 against the song's use in kindergarten hereabouts, as the daily prelude to the passing out of milk and cookies.

Spiegel somewhat wearily spelled out the basics of the constitutional separation of church and state—how it's not anti-religion but anti-hassle in intent—and how the mixing of the two "waters down religion and the worship of God" anyhow.

Spiegel had argued for the complaint at the behest of the American Civil Liberties Union, which hadn't been enthusiastic about the whole thing to begin with—"we had weightier matters to cope with"—but felt it couldn't turn down a petitioner's request.

89

The petitioner was Janet Langford, mother of two, who lives in suburban Rohnert Park, not far from Mrs. Scherba's suburb of Cotati.

Mrs. Langford moved up from San Francisco three years ago—her husband now commutes back to the city to work—with, as she said, "no feelings for or against religion, but a strong feeling about the Constitution."

Early this year, her daughter came home to report that the local school was singing "that song"—the one they'd sung in the Tiny Tots program back in San Francisco, when a phone call to the ACLU had brought an apology from the teacher involved, and discontinuance of the same "Thanksgiving" ditty's classroom use.

"I love religious music," Mr. Langford said. "I have it here in the house. But sometimes you have to take a stand, so I did, then and now."

B. Violence over Textbooks*

School Superintendent Kenneth Underwood announced last night that schools will remain closed in Kanawha County [West Virginia] "until I can be assured that students and staff can go to school without fear of violence."

Underwood issued the statement after meeting with school board members and law enforcement officials in an attempt to settle the textbook dispute that has led to violence and to picket lines at plants and mines.

The dispute began the first day of school when groups of parents protested supplemental English textbooks they said were un-American and undermined religious faith. Two persons were shot in separate incidents last week and Underwood ordered schools closed Friday.

What Do You Think?

1. If you were Judge Murphy, how would you decide the kindergarten song case? What reasons would you give for your decision?
2. To what extent do minorities in a community have to yield their beliefs to majority views?
3. Whose rights are involved in a textbook case like that in West Virginia?

7. Slowing the School Bus†

Busing to achieve racial balance is without doubt the most controversial topic in American education today. Serious violence has sometimes accompanied the inauguration of busing plans. The following editorial argues that the real problem is not busing but improving schooling for minorities.

*Associated Press, San Francisco *Chronicle,* September 16, 1974.
†From *The Wall Street Journal,* July 31, 1974. Reprinted with the permission of *The Wall Street Journal,* © Dow Jones & Company, Inc. 1974.

If the impeachment hearings hadn't occupied everyone's mind, last week's Supreme Court decision in the Detroit school desegregation case would probably have been the most widely discussed ruling of the year. Chief Justice Burger's opinion signals a major, and to our mind, much needed shift in social policy. Although headlines focused on busing, the true question was whether the business of producing an abstract numerical ratio of black and white overrode every other consideration. Justice Burger answered no, that some other things must also be weighed in the balance—in this case the integrity of local school districts if they haven't been shown to be violating law or the Constitution.

The case involved several lower court orders that would have abolished 54 local school districts in the Detroit metropolitan area for the sake of obtaining a certain proportion of the races in the Detroit city school system. The suburban districts had not been implicated in segregation, but to correct racial imbalance in Detroit, busing of some 300,000 school children would have been required. This plan was the logical outcome of absolutist reasoning on integration, which would define segregation as any situation where a public school was more than 50 percent black. But large-city systems are overwhelmingly black: more than 95 percent in Washington, D.C., and over 67 percent in Detroit itself. So you have to pull in white faces from the suburbs, dismantling school district lines.

The court, by a 5 to 4 vote, has rejected this course. As Justice Burger emphasized, local control of the schools is an important American tradition, not to be overturned lightly when there has been no proof of wrong-doing by some of the districts involved. We suspect that the emotional force of the busing issue came not from racism, but from the notion that a federal judge or bureaucrat could reach into a community, almost at random, and overturn its local school system, for no clearly stated reason except for a vague appeal to dubious social science. After all, it's hard to blame racism for George Wallace's most significant 1972 triumph, the Michigan primary by 51 percent of the vote.

The court's decision should defuse this issue, to the relief of every politician this side of Mr. Wallace. But, Thurgood Marshall to the contrary, it won't undercut enforcement of the kind of desegregation called for by *Brown v. Board of Education.* Lost in the emotional exhaust was Chief Justice Burger's explicit statement that busing was a legitimate tool to integrate a single district. Furthermore, he continued, it could be used for several districts if all of them had taken part in producing the original pattern of segregation, for instance if the districts have been deliberately gerrymandered to exclude blacks.

The judicial attack on segregation has been a noble and very worthy enterprise. Segregation, a social policy based on racial distinctions, was vicious and offensive, as well as infinitely stupid. But the attack on segregation, partly because of its judicial character, has been fixated on the source of this stupidity, concern with the racial makeup of a classroom. Instead of insuring that race is irrelevant, the goal has been to obtain a class with a fixed proportion of black and white. But of all the elements that go into learning, skin color is probably about the least important.

Detroit Mayor Coleman Young, the first black man to hold that post, was on the right track when he commented that he "shed no tears for cross-district busing." This controversy has diverted too much attention and energy from the real albeit excruciatingly difficult issue, successful teaching of impoverished minority students so that they have a real chance at breaking their "cycle of poverty." Mayor Young would concentrate on increased school financing. Others might urge curriculum reform and efficiently planned teaching programs. These measures are by no means easy or certain, but at least they are directly related to the heart of the problem, as busing is not.

We hope, finally, that the Detroit decision will be the first step in easing away from quotas, goals and the counting up of racial proportions. Such devices make sense only as a temporary and very extraordinary corrective, and this theme seems to underlie Justice Burger's decision. In the end, we have to find our way back to the principle that the Constitution is color-blind.

What Do You Think?

1. What is the main argument contained in the editorial?
2. Can you make an argument *for* busing?

ACTIVITIES FOR INVOLVEMENT

1. How can students in a school achieve good relations with neighboring householders? When conflicting sets of rights are involved—the right to move freely and the right to enjoy one's property—which right should prevail? Why?

2. Is there a bias against girls in American schools? In your school? How would you find out?

3. Prepare a questionnaire to determine what students feel about dress and other regulations in your school. What are the principal questions you would want to ask? How would you go about preparing a reliable questionnaire?

4. Prepare a dress code for boys and girls in your school. Submit it to teachers, students, and parents for their approval. Compare the responses of the three groups. What differences in acceptance do you notice? How would you explain these differences? How might you go about obtaining a wider consensus for your code among the three groups?

5. Hold a debate on the question, "Resolved: The school has no right to restrict student dress (speech, conduct, etc.) in any way."

6. Listed below are a number of possibilities for regulating teacher behavior. Which, if any, would you endorse? Why?
    • Teachers should not discuss "dangerous ideas" in the classroom.
    • Teachers should not champion unpopular causes.
    • Teachers should not hold additional jobs (that is, teachers should not "moonlight").

- Teachers should not wear loud or "improper" clothing.
- Teachers should not go on strike.
- Teachers should not be divorced.
- Teachers should not actively engage in political activity.
- Teachers should not be members of the Communist party.
- Teachers should not smoke or drink.
- Teachers should not have beards or long hair.
- Teachers should not frequent places of "ill-repute."
- Teachers should not use foul language.
- Teachers should keep their private opinions to themselves.

What would you add to the list? Why?

7. If your school does not have an up-to-date statement of students' rights and responsibilities, form a group to prepare one. Consider means of obtaining a wide range of opinion from students. How would you obtain acceptance of any such statement?

8. The following is a checklist used to evaluate "sexism" in school readers. Use it in your reading or language arts classes to judge the material used. Is it a useful list?

Evaluating Sexism in Readers

	Male	Female
1. Number of stories where main character is		
2. Number of illustrations of		
3. Number of times children are shown:		
(a) in active play		
(b) using initiative		
(c) displaying independence		
(d) solving problems		
(e) earning money		
(f) receiving recognition		
(g) being inventive		
(h) involved in sports		
(i) fearful or helpless		
(j) receiving help		
4. Number of times adults are shown:		
(a) in different occupations		
(b) playing with children		
(c) taking children on outings		
(d) teaching skills		
(e) giving tenderness		
(f) scolding children		
(g) biographically		

5. In addition, ask yourself these questions: Are boys allowed to show their emotions? Are girls rewarded for intelligence rather than for beauty? Are there any derogatory comments directed at girls in general? Is mother shown working outside the home? If so, in what kind of job? Are there any stories about one-parent families? Families without children? Are baby-sitters shown?

Carol Jacobs and Cynthia Eaton, "Evaluating Sexism in Readers," *Today's Education,* December 1972.

7
HOW MIGHT
EDUCATION
BE IMPROVED?

It is obvious that the public schools in the United States are being questioned on a number of fronts. Purposes, curriculum, administration, and procedures are all being looked at with a critical eye. As a result of the many criticisms that have appeared, many educational reformers have suggested that the public schools be modified slightly, changed drastically, or eliminated altogether. In the readings that follow, a number of suggestions for change and reform are presented. Which would you endorse? What else would you suggest?

1. Let's Change the Schools*

A school without buildings, regular teachers, or bells is described as one example in Philadelphia of an effort to make schools more meaningful for many young people. The Parkway school is one of the innovations former Superintendent Shedd took pride in developing.

If a unique concept proposed by the Board of Education here works out, the class of 1973 at a new downtown high school will have to take all day and some 20 stops to visit its alma mater.

. . . [S]tudents will attend classes in existing cultural business and scientific faculties scattered along the mile-long Benjamin Franklin Parkway northwest of City Hall. A class of 600 is expected to be added each year for three additional years.

A student might have the following class schedule:

9 A.M.   Art appreciation—the Philadelphia Museum of Art.
11 A.M.   Typing—Insurance Company of North America headquarters.
12 noon   Lunch—at the INA employee cafeteria.
2 P.M.   English—Free Library of Philadelphia.
3:30 P.M. Journalism—Philadelphia Inquirer offices.

*Excerpted from Charles Alverson, *The Wall Street Journal,* February 9, 1968. Reprinted with the permission of *The Wall Street Journal,* © Dow Jones & Company, Inc. 1968.

Other possibilities would be chemistry and biology at the Academy of Natural Science, business administration at the Bell Telephone Co. of Pennsylvania, art at the Rodin Museum, and communications at the KYW radio and television studios. The high school's administration would be at the Board of Education building.

Also named among potential participants were: The Young Men's Christian Association, the Philadelphia Bulletin, Moore College of Art, and Franklin Institute. Also mentioned was the possible use of additional space in various high-rise apartment buildings along the parkway for specialized instruction.

The idea . . . is . . . to "dramatize the fact that the schools are the community and the community the schools."

School officials stress that the new high school won't be for the elite. Two hundred of the first 600 students are to come from Central Philadelphia and the rest from outlying sections of the city and the suburbs. . . .

However, all involved spoke of the formidable logistical obstacles to be overcome. [A business] spokesman said, "We've got some dandy classrooms, but they're already on a tight timetable, and our cafeteria has a large volume now."

One possibility is that the student body of the new four-year high school may be made up of students from public, private and parochial schools. . . . The Board of Education plan also suggests creation of a special advisory board of parents, school board people, and representatives of the institutions expected to participate.

Faculty for the new high school would be drawn from the Philadelphia school system and the staffs of the institutions taking part in the plan.

What Do You Think? _____

1. Can such a program really be called a school? Why or why not?
2. How can you judge the qualifications of teachers in such an arrangement?

2. Is the "Open Classroom" the Answer?*

An increasingly popular innovation in America's schools is the "open classroom." How does it differ from traditional classrooms?

"It was good enough for us, and it's good enough for our kids," says parent X and he reminisces about how things once were. "Why, when I was 6 years old. . . ."

*Carrol Stoner, Knight Newspapers Writer, "Open Classroom—What Is It?" *San Francisco Examiner,* December 27, 1973.

"But," says Parent Y, "I want my children to have all the advantages I didn't have. ..."

Nowhere is the difficult balance of tradition/austerity vs. innovation/indulgence seen more than in education. Professional pollsters say 30 percent of all parents are opposed to change in the education of their children.

Take the open classroom. The raised voices begin with those who feel "open" means permissive and chaos; they are arrayed against those who feel "traditional" means rigid and non-readers.

How has this quiet revolution called "open classroom" taken place and imbedded itself in our American school custom? And how is it that opposition to it seems certain to fail?

It all started in the pre-Sputnik era of the mid 1950s when classrooms all sounded pretty much alike and reading, writing and arithmetic were the rule.

Then the realization that we were not at the top of the international knowledge heap dawned on America, and overnight, criticizing education became one of the hottest conversational games.

Decentralization, community control, teacher training and innovation along with integration and desegregation were the playing pieces. New approaches to teaching and learning came one on top of another. Not all worked. And some called them fads.

It was, for the average person, hard to keep up. Many traditionally involved American parents found themselves intimidated by the changes.

People who feel intimidated can become hostile. And in an era in which people are returning to traditional values in response to a barrage of negative events, it is no surprise that parents are starting to ask that their first grader be told to sit still, be quiet and learn in the same way they learned themselves. And that is not what happens in the open-style classroom.

Witness Mrs. Kircher and Miss Watson's vertical or family grouping class of kindergarten, first and second graders at a suburban Philadelphia elementary school. There are no rows or desks. Children are not sitting quietly with hands folded. There is no chorus of "Good morning, Dr. Brown." as the principal enters with a visitor.

This open classroom is not however, without order. Neither is it very noisy. There are four adults, two teachers and two helpers, scattered through the small clusters of children. Some are reading—with teachers and without —some are doing math and some are playing with puzzles.

"That one's too hard. Let's just do the easy ones," says one child to another. "No," says the other leafing through a stack of puzzles intended to teach principles of mathematics. "I like to do the hard ones. I'll teach you how."

No one approaches to remind them there is no talking. No one witnesses the exchange of information from one child to another. Open classroom advocates say this is exactly what is supposed to happen. And it does.

What, then, is the open classroom?

It is, in most cases, ungraded in the sense that children in the vertically grouped class (several grades together) are helped to learn when they show a readiness; they are not ready, then they are not pushed.

It is this non-push part of the definition that scares parents. "What if a child wants to play all day?" they ask. Open classroom advocates believe all children want to learn, but that not all 6-year-olds are ready to read at the same time. They say they will learn very easily when they are ready, and not at all when they are not.

The classroom is physically organized into interest areas—generally math, science, art and the language arts which include reading, spelling, grammar and punctuation and writing. Children move freely from one area to another.

But, ask parents, what if a child wants to draw all day? Educators answer that the teachers are still in charge. Very simply, no child would be allowed to draw all day every day.

The classroom is filled with more materials and books than you see in the traditional room.

Children are encouraged to work together regardless of ability level, so that the best students have chances to help the slower and the slower learners pick up knowledge and impetus[1] from peers. The teacher is a facilitator[2] rather than an authority figure. By all conventional standards of success—parental support, academic standards, teacher cooperation and commitment—the program seems to be working at most schools.

Even teachers who at first were horrified by the open classroom are now having second thoughts.

One suburban teacher tells of her experience in the open classroom with mixed emotions.

"We went into a new building that was built for the open-framework school. We had a new principal who had . . . no experience with our parents or our community. Parents were not informed and we were given practically no training. We had no aides—they do now—and teaching in the open classroom is really exhausting. It's much more planning time than teaching in the traditional style.

"The school district just said, 'we're going to the open system.' And that was that.

"Most of us were receptive to the idea," she says in retrospect, "but my God you just can't organize things with so little planning and expect them to work. The year was chaotic and I left. "But now they have a new principal, and things are working. In fact I hope to return to that school. I definitely feel the open classroom approach to teaching is superior to the traditional. Why? Kids learn better. And learn more. It's also more challenging and satisfying for the teacher, though as I said it's more work.

"Once you've learned to deal with the children as individuals, with different needs, you can't go back to the traditional style of teaching."

[1]Drive.
[2]One who makes learning easier.

What Do You Think?

1. Can most students handle the amount of freedom that exists in the school described in this article? Explain your reasoning.
2. Do children need more direction (or, in some cases, prodding) than this situation allows?
3. What might B. F. Skinner say about open classrooms? (Check his article in Chapter 5.)

3. What about a Year-Round School?*

As schools increasingly struggle to balance budgets, some leaders urge the adoption of year-round programs. Although often seen as a money-saving idea, the year-round school, many argue, offers distinct educational advantages as well.

Would you foul up your family's annual vacation plans too much if your children, instead of getting a long summer vacation from school, got three weeks off every couple of months? How about if they had a two-month layoff in November and December, instead of July and August?

A growing number of professional educators are betting you could adjust your plans and maybe even do it gladly. Parents of half a million kids in scores of different school districts are already in the process of adjusting. They're giving "year-round" education a try in such widely separated places as Georgia, Pennsylvania, Illinois and California, among others.

Actually, "year-round" is a misleading way to describe the experience from the student's point of view. He doesn't attend classes all year. In most cases, he gets as much vacation time as he ever did; it's just divided up differently. The school buildings are what's used virtually all year long, usually with short shutdown periods. Another name for plans that do this is "extended school year."

What's the Point?

At first, extended-year plans were simply attempts to make more efficient use of school buildings during the summer. Seeing those expensive facilities standing idle for so long was especially exasperating to school officials whose

*"Are You Ready for Year-Round Schools?", *Changing Times,* The Kiplinger Magazine, May 1974. Copyright 1974 by The Kiplinger Washington Editors, Inc., 1729 H. Street, N.W., Washington, D.C. 20006.

buildings were crowded past capacity during the academic year. Some had this thought: If the academic year could be stretched out to cover the summer, then sessions could be staggered by putting some students on vacation while others attended classes. After a couple of months or so, the vacationers would start classes and another group would start vacation. This would ease over-crowding, and maybe the district wouldn't need a new building as soon as it would under the traditional system. Taxpaying parents would be willing to put up with the inconvenience caused by the change in their children's vacation schedules because they would be spared the expense of a new school building.

School planners were thinking along these lines 70 years ago. More recent interest in the idea was sparked by the steep climb in school enrollments that has just recently begun to level off. In the meantime, plans have grown more sophisticated. Modern arguments for the extended year don't stick to the economic appeal alone. In fact some proponents have warned against expecting great savings in a school budget after adopting a year-round plan. More important, they feel, are the educational benefits that come with the change:

- School districts that switch to an extended year often redesign their curriculums to fit the new schedule. This usually means developing more and shorter courses than are called for by the traditional school calendar. Students are thus presented with a greater variety of courses from which to choose. One high school that helped pioneer the extended school year nearly tripled the number of courses it offered after making the switch.
- Students are better able to grasp the goals of shorter courses, thus teachers find it easier to maintain their interest.
- Students can't fall as far behind in a short course as they do under the semester system. If a student does flunk, he's set back only a few weeks instead of a half a year or more.
- Teachers have an opportunity to make more money. Under many plans they have the choice of a standard nine-month contract or an extended contract with a one-third increase in pay.
- There is a potential for saving money in the long run. Chiefly, savings are achieved in lowered capital expenditures for new buildings, interest on the bond issues it takes to finance them and maintenance costs that aren't incurred because fewer school board's operating budgets may actually have to increase when it shifts to year-round operations.

What Do You Think? _____

1. How would you feel about attending a year-round school?
2. What are some of the advantages of such a program?
3. What problems must be solved in implementing year-round programs?

4. "Career Ed"—A Whole New Focus for Schools*

Increasingly parents and students themselves are asking that the time spent in school have a more immediate bearing on earning a living than has been true in the past. "Vocationalism" is an old issue in American education, arising as early as 1840. As you read, compare your own educational experiences against some of the ideas discussed in the article.

Kindergarteners in Orange County, Fla., spend part of the day learning the different kinds of jobs there are caring for pets. Woven into discussion about the duties of veterinarians, animal breeders and pet store operators are lessons in identifying animals, counting them and recognizing their colors—all tied to the pet-care careers theme.

A junior high mathematics lesson in Sonoma County, Cal., is structured around banking. Students visit a local bank and interview employees about their jobs, studying the math a bank worker uses every day. Later, for English class, they write a play about getting a car loan based on their experiences, with the help of tape recordings and slides made on their trips to the bank.

At Skyline Center in Dallas, Tex., thousands of high school students from all over the city learn about careers and a variety of job-connected skills in an 80-acre complex equipped with, among other things, a million dollar computer, a color television studio and an aircraft hangar complete with planes. In all, there are courses available in more than two dozen different occupational areas—architecture, journalism, graphics and horticulture, to name a few. Each "cluster" is designed to equip students with valuable job skills even though many will choose to go on to college or technical school following graduation. Adults also use the center to sharpen old skills or learn new ones.

Public school teachers in Peoria, Ill., have written a handbook for other teachers to encourage them to work career guidance materials into their regular classes. One suggestion for second graders: A unit on restaurant jobs that includes lessons in adding up bills (for arithmetic class), restaurant jargon (for reading) and planning a well-balanced meal (science).

Examples like these barely skim the top of a national trend toward what's called "career education," possibly the most powerful thrust for change our schools have felt in years. If there's a push for it in your local schools, you could be a little confused over exactly what career education is and what it's supposed to accomplish.

Actually, there isn't a universally accepted definition or program. Sidney P. Marland Jr., career education's biggest booster when he was federal government's top education official, deliberately refused to provide a blueprint for the

"Look . . . why don't you keep hacking around for a while and come back to see me in about ten years . . . okay?"

"I appreciate your concern, but I've decided to just keep on hacking around for a while."

concept. The roots of career education, he insisted, are at the local level, and each community must work out its own program. Under Marland, the federal government supplied money for promising local projects and generally served as a national cheerleader for the idea. It also funded research designed to produce classroom materials that interested schools could use in their programs.

What career education does is reverse the traditional school timetable for demonstrating to pupils the utilitarian aspects of their education. In the past, say career ed's advocates, kids have been fed years and years of reading, writing and arithmetic before they were exposed in any systematic way to the practical applications of those subjects to their adult lives. By turning this around, by exposing kids to information about work and jobs and careers starting in the earliest years of school, you help them see the relevance of their education. the result should be stronger motivation to learn and stay in school long enough to acquire some basic skills needed to earn a living. Another result envisioned is that after exposure to a variety of options, students will realize they can come back as adults to continue their studies or prepare for a different career. Schools that don't start making this practical connection between education and jobs until their students' last couple of years miss many of the kids who need it most because they have already drifted away.

But it's not just the potential dropouts that career ed will help, its backers say. The program is also aimed at academically talented students, who often finish school with little idea of what it's like to earn a living by doing the necessary work of our society. If they're interested in a particular field of work, they're often left to find out for themselves what kind of jobs are available in it. For them, career ed will supply information and experience that widens their horizons and increases their career choices.

From Kindergarten to College

The aim of career education, then, is to equip students with what they need to make informed occupational decisions by relating much of the world of learning to the world of work. Along the way they should have opportunities to investigate a variety of jobs and to test their mental, physical and emotional capacities for handling them. How is it done? A federal government model emphasizes programs with specific objectives for different levels of schooling.

Kindergarten through sixth grade: This is called the "career awareness" phase. Children are introduced to the concept of work and jobs, the need for work and the wide variety of ways people earn a living. Lessons at first may center on the roles played by different family members, then branch out to cover the different kinds of occupation kids see represented by people who operate the school building. Policemen, firemen and other workers familiar to young children may be studied next. Ideally, information about them will be presented as part of regular classroom activities, not separate lessons. For example, alphabet drills may be a good opportunity for the teacher to point out how file clerks and others use letters to organize their work.

Seventh grade through ninth grade: "Career exploration" begins here. **103**

Students narrow down their fields of interest to three or four job clusters, which they explore in depth. As in elementary school, they read, take field trips and participate in special projects that involve "role playing" (setting up and running a simulated hotel in the classroom, for instance). Whenever possible, actual on-the-job experience supplied by cooperating local businesses and other organizations is added at this level. By the time they finish junior high school, students should have a good idea of the types of jobs that interest them and be able to make a tentative choice of one or more that interest them the most.

High school: Students now begin to acquire actual job skills in these fields. Training in typing, auto mechanics, electronics, drafting and other skills that can be taught at the high school level is made available to everyone, even students who intend to go to college. At this level a large part of a career education becomes what is usually called "vocational" education. The idea is to give all students an opportunity to pursue training and study that could lead directly to a job after high school or to further training and study at a technical institute, business school, or two- or four-year college and beyond.

Obviously, then, career education isn't just a new course that schools are teaching. It's supposed to cut across all courses. Its strongest proponents originally advocated rewriting the entire curriculum from top to bottom in order to accommodate the career ed concept. Now, though, it appears the approach will be less ambitious and probably rely on the development of various lesson plans that can be plugged in to existing curriculums.

Not Everybody's a Fan

"The latest example of education's search for the magic answer" is one critic's estimate of career education. Good teachers have always tried to relate classroom lessons to situations outside the classroom, she says, especially job and career choices. Career education is just a new name for an old idea that, this critic fears, can't possibly fulfill the expectations the public is being given for it.

Other critics say career ed forces kids to start narrowing down their career options too early in their lives, putting them on a track many will want to get off a few years later. Still others express the fear that the movement is basically anti-intellectual and will sacrifice a well-rounded academic approach to education for a program designed merely "to get people into jobs and to condition them to a life in the marketplace," as one strong critic put it. Other critics say that the record of vocational education indicates that school-sponsored programs aren't very successful in preparing students to get jobs.

Political issues are involved too. Foremost is the struggle for government funding among the advocates of career education and backers of other programs who are afraid the money will be shifted away from them. Finally, there is the question of whether funding for the massive programs needed to provide career ed training for teachers and administrators is a realistic expectation. Already the federal government has begun to pull back from its earlier plans, content to let this year be one of evaluation instead of expansion of the program.

So will career education fade away or will it continue to spread? There are indications that, at the least, the momentum is strong enough to carry it into many more school districts. For one thing, most of the instructional materials now being used have been developed at the local level, often on local initiative independent of federal funding or guidance. That takes grass-roots commitment. State education departments have also displayed a willingness to spend money to develop programs. Much of the push for career ed started at the local level. If the federal government's drive to coordinate the movement falls apart, there's little reason to think career education will die as a result.

How Career Ed Works in the Classroom

Here's how a group of teachers in Peoria, Ill., Public School District 150 suggests a career ed unit on jobs in a department store might be integrated into the regular subjects taught in third and fourth grades. Occupations covered include manager, cashier, stock person, delivery person, clerk, security guard, gift wrapper, buyer and advertising manager.

Suggested activities for children in each class:

Reading: Read stories that are related to department stores in basic readers, supplementary books and library books.

Language arts: List vocabulary words used in a department store. Take notes on a visit by someone who works for a local store. Interview workers and take notes during a field trip to a store. Give oral reports on occupations in department stores.

Mathematics: Make out a sales slip. Figure out profit and loss. Make change. Figure the best buy in a particular piece of merchandise by comparing prices in advertisements. Use multiplication and division in figuring the cost of a single item from a group price and vice versa.

Social studies: Study the origin and transportation of various products. Study the international relationships and the people of countries represented by the products in a department store.

Science: Determine the correct content labels for various items in a store. Under supervision, test flammable and fire-resistant articles.

Art: Make labels for a store. Design an advertisement. Make a collage depicting an aspect of department store operation. Make art paper and use it to gift wrap articles from a store.

Class project: Set up, name and operate a store in the classroom. Articles may be miniatures, such as toys, or pictures cut from magazines.

What Do You Think? _____

1. Would your education be more valuable to you if it had more concern with future careers? What changes could be made to accomplish that aim?

2. Are there dangers in concentrating early in life on career preparation? Do the programs outlined in the article avoid those dangers?

---

5. A "Speed-Up" in Education—It's About Time*

Some educators feel that the time spent in schools is too long for many students. The National Commission on Reform of Secondary Education has what they think is a solution for some students—an earlier school-leaving age.

Before the decade is over, many 14-year olds may no longer have to worry about passing the next science examination. That's because Johnny may be at work, or down the street learning about science from an ex-school teacher, or delaying his education for a couple of years to study Chopin.

*From Dennis Chase, "Your World Tomorrow—Schools Are Downgraded," San Francisco *Chronicle,* Monday, April 18, 1974. Reprinted by permission of McGraw-Hill World News. © 1974 World News/McGraw-Hill, Inc.

As dissatisfaction with school performance spreads and student dropouts increase, education critics are zeroing in on a new target: universal, compulsory school attendance. They say compulsory attendance is unnecessary, undesirable, unenforceable, and may be unconstitutional.

"Compulsory schooling certainly has not made us rush to provide alternative programs to meet the educational requirements of all the American youths," David L. Moberly, superintendent of the Cleveland Heights-University Heights school pointed out to the district convention of the American Association of School Administrators in February.

But the biggest blast came last December when the National Commission on the Reform of Secondary Education recommended that courts recognize "the right (of American students) not to be in formal school beyond the age of 14." It called compulsory attendance laws a "dead hand" on high schools.

Then last month Phi Delta Kappa, the national educational fraternity, called together a group of educators and state officials in Denver to decide how to tackle the issue. They plan to set up a special group to analyze the question of whether compulsory attendance laws should be modified by lowering the age to 14, or maybe lower than that.

The groups will have a lot of charges and counter-charges to analyze. Critics of compulsory school attendance point out that most parents encourage their children to enroll in school but students who don't want to be in school simply don't show up. Those who do create havoc for the rest.

A recent report called "Super Parent," by University of Chicago education professor Donald Erickson, calls for the elimination of compulsory attendance laws in order to improve the public school system.

"Within such a framework of freedom," Erickson writes, "We should seldom encounter examples as we often do today of potential Chopins who must leave their pianos to participate in what is for them an inane classroom discussion of Baroque music, of Olympic skating champions whose high school graduation diplomas are held up for lack of physical education credits, and of many other children who could learn inestimably more of what is important and useful to them in settings that the law now makes generally inaccessible during the prolonged periods of compulsory attendance."

Yet there are powerful voices opposed to change, including National Education Association and American Federation of Teachers.

By Autumn, the proposed study group likely will be tackling the issue head-on and could very well devise "model" or "sample" legislation for all 50 states. Another possibility is that the group will meet with labor organizations to persuade them to modify child labor and minimum wage laws so that 14–16-year olds can work at school-approved jobs, if they wish, and earn a special "learner's wage."

"We're not going to propose eliminating the (compulsory attendance) laws before we have a pretty firm base on alternatives," said Stanley Elam, who represents the Phi Delta Kappa board of directors in Bloomington, Ind. "But the idea that all kids should go through the same hoop is changing." **107**

Which direction the group might go is uncertain. German and Swedish apprenticeship-type programs are a possibility, where schools work "hand-in-glove" with business and industry. Elam says the group could propose a "voucher" plan where students could use the vouchers for education at any time in their lives, perhaps even in schools set up in factories. Said Elam. "We're starting to realize that certain kids would be better off not cooped up within four walls."

What Do You Think? _____

1. Can time be saved in the typical American pattern of four years of high school and four years of college?

2. In your own experience, where might some time have been saved? Where might more time have been added?

3. Do you think youngsters should leave school at fourteen, even if not performing well? If so, should there be any plans for further education in other settings?

---

6. Alleviation from the Trap*

Some far-out "suggestions" from a noted critic of schools.

The compulsory system has become a universal trap, and it is no good. Very many, and perhaps most, of the youth—both underprivileged and middle-class—might be better off if the system did not exist, even if they then had no formal schooling at all. But what would become of them? For very many —both underprivileged and middle-class—their homes are worse then the schools, and the streets are worse in another way. Our urban and suburban environments are precisely not cities or communities where adults attend to the young and educate to a viable life. Also, perhaps especially in the case of the overt dropouts, the state of their body and soul is such that we must give them some refuge and remedy—whether it be called school, youth work, work camp, or settlement house.

This is not the place for a long list of practical proposals to make the schools worth attending. However, it is relevant to offer a few ideas toward the main subject . . . the system as a compulsory trap. In principle, when a law begins to do more harm than good, the best policy is to alleviate it. I would suggest the following experiments:

*Excerpted from Paul Goodman, "The Universal Trap," *The School Dropout,* Daniel Schreiber (ed.) (Washington, D.C.: National Education Association, 1964), pp. 40–53.

1. Have "no school at all" for a few classes. These children should be selected from tolerable, though not necessarily cultured, homes. They should be numerous enough and neighborly enough to be a society for one another. Will they learn the rudiments anyway? The experiment could not harm them, since there is evidence (Sloan Wayland) that normal children can make up the first six or seven years with a few months of good teaching.

2. Largely dispense with the school building for a few classes, and use the city itself as a school—the streets, cafeterias, stores, movies, museums, parks, and factories. Such a class should probably not exceed 10 children for 1 pedagogue. The idea (an Athenian one) is not dissimilar to youth gang work, though not employing delinquents nor playing to the gang ideology.

3. Along the same lines, but both outside and inside the school, use appropriate adults of the community—such as the druggist, the storekeeper, the mechanic—as the proper educators of the young into the grown-up world. By this means, it would be possible to overcome the separation of the young from the grown-up world in our urban life and to diminish the omnivorous authority of the school. This experience would be useful and animating for the adults. (We have begun a volunteer program along these lines in New York City.)

Students visit the Museum of Modern Art in New York City. **109**

4. Make class attendance not compulsory (A. S. Neill). If the teachers are good, absence should soon be eliminated. The reason for the compulsory law is to get the children from the parents, but it must not be a trap for the children. A modification might be permission to spend a week or a month in any worthwhile enterprise or environment (Frank Brown).
5. Decentralize the school into small units of perhaps 100—in clubhouses —combining play, social activity, discussion, and formal teaching. Special events could bring together the many small units to a common auditorium or gymnasium so as to give the sense of the greater community.
6. For a couple of months of the school year, send children to farms to take part in the farm life, perhaps two or three children to a farmer. This would serve to give the farmer cash, as part of a generally desirable program to redress the urban-rural ratio to something nearer to 70–30.

Above all, apply these or any other proposals to particular individuals or small groups, without the obligation of uniformity. There is a case for uniform standards of achievement, but they cannot be reached by uniform techniques. The claim that standardization of procedure is more efficient, less costly, or alone administratively practical is usually false. Particular inventiveness requires thought, but thought does not cost money. And the more the authority to initiate is delegated to many, the wiser and freer we will be.

What Do You Think?_____

Would all (or any) of these suggestions work? Which seem most practicable? Why?

---

7. How the Schools Can Make a Difference*

The next reading urges the adoption by schools of a "critical approach" to learning. What does this mean?

Educators and educational institutions have helped to improve the quality of life in our society by helping to advance knowledge, promote health, elevate morals, and increase aesthetic[1] sensitivity. Moreover, they have helped to improve the social, economic, and political arrangements of our society. Now these are no mean accomplishments. Yet, all about us, accusations erupt: the schools are failing; schools are irrelevant; they make no difference.

Why this diffidence?[2] Why this loss of faith in the power of education? Let me suggest an hypothesis.

*From Henry J. Perkinson, "How the Schools Can Make a Difference," *Intellect,* March 1974.
[1]Appreciative of art and beauty.
[2]Lack of confidence.

First, however, we might ask why Americans have had this faith in the power of the schools? Historically, this stems from the fact that, in the beginning, America was a new land, a new society, lacking established institutions, set roles, and patterns for all. In this open land of opportunity, the schools took on functions beyond those traditionally assigned to their counterparts in Europe. Later, when this new society gave birth to the first new nation, Americans expected the schools to maintain and protect their newly won liberty.

After the Civil War, Americans faced a host of new problems generated by the emancipation of the slaves, the industrialization of work, the urbanization of the population, and the nationalization of government. However, instead of dealing directly with these problems, most Americans converted them into educational problems and asked the schools to solve them. They expected the schools to promote racial harmony, overcome urban alienation, insure equality of opportunity, and assuage[3] the fears of big government. This ploy[4] not only allowed them to evade these problems, it also provided someone to blame when the situation got worse.

This pattern continues. Many Americans still convert social, political, and economic problems into educational ones, assign schools the responsibility for solving them, and then blame educators when things deteriorate. Do we have a population explosion?—then let us supply sex education in the schools. Are we worried about pollution?—let the schools teach ecology. Frightened by drug addiction?—the schools will conduct drug education programs. Unemployment?—provide career education. Supply your own crisis and somebody will prescribe the educational nostrum[5] for it.

Although this habitual faith in the power of the schools persists, recent events have seriously undermined it in many quarters. One immediately thinks of the sobering reports from James Coleman and Christopher Jencks[6] documenting the impotence of our educational enterprise to effect significant social change. Yet, these investigations merely supply scientific sanction to an erosion of faith already brought about when some people, plagued by unbearable social conditions, turned to direct action to redress the wrongs they suffered. This long-standing faith in the power of the schools had provided a safety valve for the society—the schools offered the promise of peaceful change and improvement. However—at the moment people demanded immediate improvement, refused to wait for educational remedies, and directly confronted what oppressed them—they discovered that our existing arrangements lack sufficient institutional means to solve the problems. In the very act of discovering this, many now saw the schools in a new light—as agencies to manipulate, to co-opt, to mystify people; as agencies to adjust and accommodate people to the *status quo.*

These discoveries brought on a loss of faith in the traditional schools of the establishment. Yet, many of those now disenchanted with the existing schools continued to maintain a faith in the idea that schools—rightly con-

[3]Lessen.
[4]Action to outwit.
[5]Remedy.
[6]Two critical observers of schools.

structed—could work *for* people, not *against* them. So, while some tried to gain control and to turn around the establishment schools, others moved on to alternative or free schools that would make a difference by liberating people, not oppressing them. These free schools have appeared in urban ghettos, in the woods of Vermont, and in the mountains of Colorado.

Still other Americans have now lost faith in all schools. They are convinced that no schools, not even alternative schools, effect any significant social change; that schools are irrelevant—they could never make a difference.

In recent years, we have witnessed a loss of faith—in some cases, in "establishment schools"; in others, in all schools. Crises of faith are infectious, and educators are not immune. Hence their diffidence and uneasiness: "How can the schools make a difference?"

By now, of course, my hypothesis is obvious: People think that the schools have failed because they have expected, and continue to expect, too much from them.

These great expectations have led educators to a couple of false assumptions. First, educators have had to assume that we possess wisdom enough to know the answers to the social, political, and economic problems that beset us. We have never possessed such wisdom—at no time did we have the answers. We are not omniscient,[7] not gods, but, simply, fallible[8] human beings. Yet, once we had assumed we had the answers, we then moved to our second faulty assumption—that our central concern as educators is the delivery of the answers. In other words, our second assumption was that our educational task is purely technical. Technical matters have absorbed most of our attention: the correct patterns of school organization, the right packaging of the curriculum, sure-fire teaching methods.

Common sense tells us that, if we are not omniscient—if we do not have the answers to our social, political, and economic problems—then questions of how to go about delivering them are just irrelevant. Thus, educators, I think, must shift their attention away from these technical concerns to basic questions about the functions of the school. In addition, if I am correct about human fallibility, we should develop functions that are in accord with our human condition.

Let me suggest what the social function of the school might be. Looking about at our politics, economy, and social order, we can see that they are not perfect since they were created by imperfect human beings. Yet, they are not totally without merit, and they can be improved. Accordingly, here is my recommendation for how schools can make a difference—schools can take on the function of helping to improve the existing political, social, and economic arrangements. Instead of asking the young to accept and give thanks for being beneficiaries of them, the schools should take on the conscious and deliberate task of equipping the young to help improve them.

[7]Having infinite knowledge.
112 [8]Capable of error.

If one is serious about improvement, he can do no better than to look at the example of man's most glorious creation—science. How did man improve his knowledge of the universe? How did he advance beyond notions like those of Thales, who taught that "the earth is supported by water on which it rides like a ship, and when we say that there is an earthquake, then the earth is being shaken by the movement of water."

There is no mystery about how we improved our knowledge of the universe we inhabit. We improved our knowledge by developing a critical approach toward it. Thus, Anaximander, Thales' pupil, did not accept his teacher's theory. He criticized it and came up with a better one. Thus, throughout the history of science, men have advanced knowledge by criticizing the existing knowledge and then refining it in the light of successful criticism.

We can, and do, improve our social arrangements in the same way—criticize them and change them in the light of unrefuted criticism. It is rare to find a conscious and deliberate program to criticize the existing arrangements, although Socrates took on a program not unlike what I am suggesting. Devoted to the improvement of his country and his countrymen, he went about continually raising criticisms. Yet, we all know what happened to Socrates. As a colleague once pointed out to me, gadflies get swatted.

Here is where the school comes in. Socrates was the victim of the absence of a critical tradition in Greece. The Athenians, like most, practiced the dogmatic[9] preservation of the *status quo*. The schools today can begin to create a critical tradition by presenting our present social arrangements as imperfect, created by fallible men. Teachers can encourage students to study them and then to criticize them. At that point, the teacher's role will be that of a critic of the students' criticism. For frankly, much of the students' criticisms will be unfounded, misguided, or mistaken. However, the teacher can enter into dialogue with them and he can demonstrate that all criticism is not equally good. To be good, criticism must be able to withstand countercriticism.

Because our present education now lacks such critical encounters, the young do not understand the existing social, political, and economic arrangements, and they do not know how to use them to protect themselves. They feel alienated from, and victimized by, the present system, which they see as unchangeable—except perhaps by force.

Because we have not yet begun to create this critical tradition, those who do seek change do not look for dialogue, but for confrontation. Without this critical tradition, all of us become more cynical and powerless in the face of arbitrary, even tyrannical, exercise of power by those who occupy positions of authority in our various institutions.

* * * * *

The improvement of society is up to its adult members, who must be critical of what is going on. The schools can play a modest role by helping to

[9]By decree.

create critical citizens, critical workers, critical consumers, critical neighbors. We do not aim to create a corps of carpers,[10] ready to complain about and tear down whatever displeases them, but, rather, critics who are self-critical and open, ready to engage in critical dialogue in order to improve things.

What I am suggesting contains little that is new. Schools have always helped to improve things by making people critical. Even when schools consciously sought to indoctrinate the young and, thus, to preserve the *status quo,* they usually wound up making people critical. Education, with its own dynamic and its own logic, is inherently subversive. An educated person will think, and criticize. This places all that exists in jeopardy. What is new in my suggestion is that we must consciously and deliberately encourage criticism, developing it through critical dialogue into a critical approach that seeks to improve, not destroy.

This proposal is not a call for schools or teachers to be advocates of a particular ideology or point of view. It *is* a call for the schools to become centers of criticism, where all that exists and all proposals for change are open to critical examination.

The schools can do more. They can make a modest contribution to the improvement of our society, as well as to that of each individual student. They can use the critical approach to improve the ideas and skills the students already have. Thus, the schools would take the students' ideas and skills seriously, subjecting them to criticism, allowing the students to refine and change them in the light of criticism. This is not to abandon the traditional subject matter, but to use it to evoke and elicit the talents the students already possess, rather than to try to impose it on them. Focusing on what the students already know and what they can do, teachers can help them—through criticism—to recognize its inadequacies, allowing them to change and refine it.

The functions proposed here are rooted in the recognition of human fallibility. We have no wisdom to impart, no answers to supply to our students. We have an existing society and traditional bodies of knowledge. Our students must be let in on the not-too-well-kept secret that neither our society nor our knowledge is perfect, but, simultaneously, they must be given the glad tidings that all can be improved. Our function can be to initiate them into the human enterprise of improving our knowledge and our society through criticism and through refinement in the light of criticism. This is a modest expectation of what the schools can do, but it is a noble endeavor.

What Do You Think? _____

1. How would students feel about the author's suggestion for having the schools make a difference? How do you feel?

2. What burdens might his suggestion place on teachers? On administrators? Would most teachers and administrators tend to favor the author's ideas?

114   [10]Petty fault-finders.

3. To what extent do schools perform a critical function now?
4. Are education and schooling one and the same? If not, how do they differ?
5. What, to you, should be the major purpose of education?

ACTIVITIES FOR INVOLVEMENT

1. Review any of the readings in this chapter. What weaknesses might critics point out about the proposal offered? How would you answer these critics?

2. Read the description below. Imagine that you have been asked to design a course of study for these individuals. What would you argue as having *highest* priority? Explain.

WHO ARE THE HARD-CORE UNEMPLOYED?[1]

Nobody knows how many persons in the United States fit into this category.

We do know that there are about 10 million adults and older youths who are *"functional illiterates."* They are out of work, on welfare, or in dead-end jobs.

- They cannot comprehend the help-wanted jobs.
- They cannot read street signs to get to work.
- They cannot fill out a job application.
- Another way to approach the question is to look at the basis used by government agencies to determine the hard core. Included are individuals who are
  (a) School dropouts.
  (b) Less than 22 years old.
  (c) Over 45 years of age.
  (d) Physically or mentally handicapped.
  (e) Subject to special obstacles to employment.
  (f) Unskilled or service workers whose periods of unemployment during the past year exceed fifteen weeks.
  (g) Workers with descending job status.
  (h) Long-term welfare recipients.
  (i) Laid off permanently in declining industries; e.g., coal mining.
  (j) Members of minority groups.

Their motivation is generally poor, and so is their health. Many are impeded by language barriers, beset by family troubles, or blocked by prejudice.

3. Suppose you had as much money as you needed to establish an *ideal* school. What characteristics would such a school possess?

[1] Excerpted from *"Christopher News Notes,"* March 1969.

4. The cartoon below suggests a great deal about educational experimentation. Why have so few experiments lasted? Why is genuine and lasting change so difficult to bring about?

"I was lucky enough to be a product of one of the more successful educational experiments."

© Punch—ROTHKO.

BIBLIOGRAPHY
For Further Study

BOOKS

ACKERMAN, NATHAN W. • *Summerhill: For and Against* • New York, N.Y.: Hart Publishing Co., 1970.

BEREITER, CARL • *Must We Educate?* • Englewood Cliffs, N.J.: Prentice-Hall, Inc., 1973.

BROWN, B. FRANK • *The Reform of Secondary Education* • New York, N.Y.: McGraw-Hill Book Co., Inc., 1973.

CASS, JAMES (ed.) • *The Great Contemporary Issues: Education, U.S.A.* • New York, N.Y.: Arno Press, 1973.

CORWIN, RICHARD G. • *Education in Crisis: A Sociological Analysis of Schools and Universities in Transition* • New York, N.Y.: John Wiley & Sons, Inc., 1974.

HUMMEL, RAYMOND C., and NAGLE, JOHN M. • *Urban Education in America* • New York, N.Y.: Oxford University Press, 1973.

KROLL, ARTHUR M. (ed.) • *Issues in American Education* • New York, N.Y.: Oxford University Press, 1970.

MILLS, NICOLAUS • *The Great School Bus Controversy* • New York, N.Y.: Teachers College Press, 1973.

SILBERMAN, CHARLES • *Crisis in the Classroom* • New York, N.Y.: Random House, 1970.

SOWELL, THOMAS • *Black Education: Myths and Tragedies* • New York, N.Y.: David McKay Co., Inc., 1972.

PERKINSON, HENRY J. • *The Imperfect Panacea: American Faith in Education* • New York, N.Y.: Random House, 1968.

WOODRING, PAUL • *Introduction to American Education* • New York, N.Y.: Harcourt, Brace & World, Inc., 1965.

PAPERBACKS

EHLERS, HENRY (ed.) • *Crucial Issues in Education* • New York, N.Y.: Holt, Rinehart, and Winston, 1973.

HOLT, JOHN • *Freedom and Beyond* • New York, N.Y.: Delta, 1972.

JAMES, CHARITY • *Young Lives at Stake: The Education of Adolescents* • New York, N.Y.: Schocken Books, Inc., 1973.

JENCKS, CHRISTOPHER • *Inequality: A Reassessment of the Effect of Family and Schooling in America* • New York, N.Y.: Harper & Row Publishers, Inc., 1973.

KOZOL, JONATHAN • *Free Schools* • Boston, Mass.: Bantam Books, 1972.

LEVINE, ALAN H. • *The Rights of Students* • New York, N.Y.: Avon Books Div., 1973.

POSTMAN, NEIL, and WEINGARTNER, CHARLES • *Teaching as a Subversive Activity* • New York, N.Y.: Delta, 1971.

117

PRATTE, RICHARD • *The Public School: A Critical Study* • New York, N.Y.: David McKay Co., Inc., 1973.

SILBERMAN, CHARLES E. • *The Open Classroom Reader* • New York, N.Y.: Vintage Books, Inc., 1973.

SOWELL, THOMAS • *Black Education: Myths and Tragedies* • New York, N.Y.: David McKay Co., Inc., 1972.

TOFFLER, ALVIN • *Learning for Tomorrow: The Role of the Future in Education* • New York, N.Y.: Random House, Inc., 1974.

WILLIAMS, SYLVIA BERRY • *Hassling* • Boston, Mass.: Little, Brown and Co., 1970.

ARTICLES

ARONS, STEPHEN • "Compulsory Education; The Plain People Resist," *Saturday Review,* January 15, 1972.

BELL, TERREL H. • "Is School Busing at a Dead End?" *U.S. News & World Report,* September 16, 1974.

BUXTON, T. H., and PRICHARD, K. W. • "Student Perceptions of Teacher Violations of Human Rights," *Phi Delta Kappan,* September 1973.

CASS, JAMES • "Schools in Perspective," *Saturday Review,* February 1973.

GREELEY, ANDREW M. • "Public and Nonpublic Schools—Losers Both," *School Review,* February 1973.

KNOLES, LAURENCE W. • "Faculty Free Speech: Old Mores Crumble Under New Legal Liberality of Recent Court Rulings," *Nation's Schools,* May 1970.

LIEBERMAN, MYRON • "The Union Merger Movement: Will 3,5000,000 Teachers Put It All Together?" *Saturday Review,* June 24, 1972.

McLUHAN, MARSHALL, and LEONARD, GEORGE B. • "The Future of Education: The Class of 1989," *Look,* February 21, 1967.

MALLIOS, HARRY C. • "Symbolic Expression: The New Battle Facing School Administrators," *Intellect,* November 1972.

MARIN, PETER • "Has Imagination Outstripped Reality: The Free School Nonmovement," *Saturday Review,* July 1972.

SALZ, ARTHUR E., and SMITH, MORTIMER • "The Truly Open Classroom" and "Before and After the Truly Open Classroom," *Phi Delta Kappan,* February 1974.

FILMS

A Chance to Learn (17 min; B/W; prod. NBC TV) Studies Rochester's approach to divisive problems of public education in the inner city. Answers questions: Who shall control? Who shall decide who teaches and what is taught.

Dropout (28 min; B/W; prod. International Film Bureau) • The story of youngsters who leave high school before graduation. Indicates how a community can tackle the dropout problem through special programs such as work experience and remedial reading.

Hickory Stick (28 min; B/W; prod. International Film Bureau) • How a fifth-grade teacher maintains an orderly atmosphere for learning and at the same time provides youngsters with help in coping with their behavior and learning problems.

James B. Conant (30 min; B/W; prod. Encyclopædia Britannica Films) • A conversation between the former President of Harvard University and Ambassador to Germany, James B. Conant, and Nathaniel Ober, principal of Clayton, Missouri High School about the critical problems of American education. Dr. Conant and Mr. Ober surveyed fifty schools together in 1958 in connection with a study of the American public high school for the Carnegie Foundation. The conclusions of the survey are discussed in the film.

Joe and Roxy (27 min; B/W; prod. International Film Bureau) • Focus of the film is on the many problems which face today's teen-ager: going steady; planning for a future in an ever-changing world; seeing education as a significant factor in assuring a satisfying life; learning to make necessary adjustments best to cope with daily living. Emphasis is on the importance of the home to satisfactory adjustment.

Maintaining Classroom Discipline (14 min; B/W; prod. McGraw-Hill) • Concerned with techniques for securing proper class conduct and attitude. Although designed for teacher training, the film stimulates student thinking and discussion on the issue of behavior and control in the classroom.

No Reason to Stay • (28 min; B/W; prod. National Film Board of Canada) • Written by a high school dropout. Explains why intelligent young people drop out of high school. Emphasis on the problem of school and able, dissatisfied youth.

Parents and College (30 min; B/W; prod. NET Film Service) • Parents and guidance counselors discuss problems faced when young people make the transition from high school to college.

Sixteen in Webster Groves (47 min; B/W; Carousel Films) • Attitudes of sixteen-year-olds toward parents, school, marriage, and their future are the focus of this film. Stimulates discussion of many educational issues, including the factor of bias in the mass media. The narrator does not explain that the somber-faced young people in one segment of the film were leaving the funeral of one of their friends.

Teacher Gap (60 min; B/W; prod. NET Film Service) • Examines the quality of teaching in the public school as well as the shortage of teachers. Show how two communities with differing attitudes regarding the importance of education differ on financial support for schools and the quality and success of the educational programs. Interviews and discussions with teachers, politicians, and education leaders are provocative.

Teens (26 min: B/W; prod. McGraw-Hill) • Focuses on the out-of-school life of three teen-agers in an urban middle-class setting. Encourages discussion of the place of school in a young persons total life experience.

What Price Education (14 min; color; prod. Handy) • Re-enact's Alphonse Daudet's "The Last Lesson." Emphasizes the value of using learning opportunities before they are lost by telling the story of a young Alsatian boy who wasted his school years and then lost any further opportunity when the German army arrived in his home town.

Young Americans (60 min; B/W; prod. NET Film Service) • What do the youth of today want, how do they affect society, and in what do they believe—those are the questions raised in this film. Young Americans are viewed in a variety of settings, including schools, in an effort to depict "youth culture." A frankly provocative film that offers no answers but encourages serious questioning. Includes Peace Corps volunteers, college civil rights workers in the South, and young political activists. **119**

FILMSTRIPS

Education (Battle for Liberty Series; 68 fr; B/W; prod. Handy) • Presents group discussions to stimulate a positive philosophy of freedom as related to education. A 33⅓ rpm record accompanies.

Education for All American Children (47 fr.; B/W; prod. NEA) • Defines U.S. goals in education and the roles of administrator, teacher, and the community.

Education in a Democracy (26 fr; color; prod. NYT) • Examines the relation of education to good citizenship.

Education in the Big City (40 fr; color; prod. EGH) • Focuses on the critical relation of education to the life of the city.